TEACHING WITH SUPERPOWERS

This book is dedicated to

my sister, Karin, whose superpowered inspiration birthed this book;

my children, Randy and Holly, whose amazing superpowers are a force for good in the world; and

my love, David, whose superpowered love for me brings me joy and delight!

TEACHING WITH SUPERPOWERS
Ten Brain-Informed Practices

C. Bobbi Hansen

For information:

Corwin
A Sage Company
2455 Teller Road
Thousand Oaks, California 91320
(800) 233-9936
www.corwin.com

Sage Publications Ltd.
1 Oliver's Yard
55 City Road
London EC1Y 1SP
United Kingdom

Sage Publications India Pvt. Ltd.
Unit No 323-333, Third Floor, F-Block
International Trade Tower Nehru Place
New Delhi 110 019
India

Sage Publications Asia-Pacific Pte. Ltd.
18 Cross Street #10-10/11/12
China Square Central
Singapore 048423

Vice President and Editorial Director:
  Monica Eckman
Publisher: Jessica Allan
Content Development Editor:
  Mia Rodriguez
Production Editor: Vijayakumar
Copy Editor: Colleen Brennan
Typesetter: TNQ Tech Pvt. Ltd.
Proofreader: Girish Sharma
Indexer: TNQ Tech Pvt. Ltd.
Cover Designer: Scott Van Atta
Marketing Manager: Stephanie Trkay

Printed in the United States of America

Library of Congress Cataloging-in-Publication Data

Names: Hansen, C. Bobbi, author.

Title: Teaching with superpowers : ten brain-informed practices / Bobbi Hansen, University of San Diego.

Description: Thousand Oaks, California : Corwin Press, [2024] | Includes bibliographical references and index.

Identifiers: LCCN 2024012470 | ISBN 9781071904411 (paperback) | ISBN 9781071904442 (adobe pdf) | ISBN 9781071904428 (epub) | ISBN 9781071904435 (epub)

Subjects: LCSH: Learning, Psychology of. | Cognitive neuroscience. | Educational psychology.

Classification: LCC LB1060 .H3459 2024 | DDC 370.15/23--dc23/20240417eng/20231117

LC record available at https://lccn.loc.gov/2024012470

This book is printed on acid-free paper.

24 25 26 27 28 10 9 8 7 6 5 4 3 2 1

TABLE OF CONTENTS

PREFACE

To all who have chosen to read this book, thank you! Information in this book rests on the hard work and inspiration of hundreds of (mostly) 21st-century psychologists, neuroscientists, and educational researchers. I would like to acknowledge that I am not the first educator to become excited by the extraordinary possibilities that new research on the brain can bring to the teaching/learning arena. I believe I am, however, the first to propose that teachers who center their classroom instructional practices on these new findings have, in a manner of speaking, SUPERPOWERS and a distinct advantage in enhancing their students' learning.

AUTHOR ACKNOWLEDGMENTS

I would like to acknowledge the many superheroes who brought this book to life beginning with **Jessica Allan**, Publisher, Corwin. I am extremely grateful for her creative support of the vision for this book; she is a pleasure to work with and a constant source of optimism. Also, I would like to thank both **Lucas Schleicher, Content Development Manager,** and **Mia Rodriguez, Content Development Editor,** who guided and navigated my journey from inception to final production, and **Natalie Delpino, Senior Editorial Assistant,** for your work. Finally, thank you to **Colleen Brennan**, who copyedited the manuscript and whose astute, meticulous eye helped get the text in the form needed for publication. And to all others who assisted in the process, know that I very much appreciate the integral role you played in the production of this book.

Next, I would like to honor the dozens of researchers and writers whose work has been mentioned in this book. Without your wisdom, hard work, and willingness to share your knowledge with the larger educational community, this book could not have been written.

Finally, thank you to my students, past, present, and future, for allowing me the privilege of joining you in our learning communities so that we may better meet the academic, social, and emotional needs of all of the PK–12 students entrusted to our care.

PUBLISHER'S ACKNOWLEDGMENTS

Corwin gratefully acknowledges the contributions of the following reviewers:

Debi Gartland
Professor of Special Education
Towson University
Towson, Maryland

Ernie Rambo
Education Consultant
Transformative Education Consulting
Las Vegas, NV

Deborah Smith
Instructional Coach
Beaufort Elementary School
Beaufort, SC

ABOUT THE AUTHOR

Dr. C. Bobbi Hansen is an associate professor at the University of San Diego, where she was twice awarded university honors in teaching, scholarship, and service. Additionally, in 2017, she was named San Diego Science Educator of the Year for excellence in university science teaching. Dr. Hansen considers herself first a learner, then a teacher as she instructs preservice through graduate-level teacher education courses. Her passion is assisting teachers to better understand and utilize instructional practices that are centered on new advances in the educational neurosciences.

Dr. Hansen has previously authored or co-authored three books and numerous articles focusing on transformative instructional practices. Having been invited to speak at national and international events, she has shared this compelling information with hundreds of educators. Her message is that every one of us has billions-upon-billions of brain cells and an incalculable capacity for learning. As teachers, we are in a privileged position to convey this affirmative evidence to our students and help them uncover their unique learning capacities and talents.

INTRODUCTION

Educational neuroscience for all
means changing our practice so that we make the
fundamental shift from "doing school" to learning.
–Whitman and Kelleher (2016)

Superheroes are everywhere—in the movies, comic books, the internet, cereal boxes, kids' clothing, and even classrooms! Yes, teachers can be superheroes, too! The question becomes, then, what makes a superhero? From Superman to Spider-Man, Captain Marvel, the Hulk, and even a Jedi Knight, their superpowers are a defining characteristic.

Now, let's return to the matter of becoming a superhero teacher. Researchers in educational neuroscience, a burgeoning new field integrating brain science, cognitive psychology, and education, are beginning to discover what happens in the human brain as it learns. This book was written so that you may unleash your inner teacher-superhero as you use these potent teaching/learning principles and claim them as your very own *superpowers!*

Using a lighthearted format, this book will identify 10 categories of superpowers you may activate to optimize how your students' brains take in, process, and store information.

Most of us can easily recount the superpowers attributed to the world's favorite superhero, Superman: "faster than a speeding bullet, stronger than a locomotive, able to leap tall buildings in a single bound." Similarly, when speaking about educational neuroscience, Tokuhama-Espinosa (2011) shares this playful analogy: "Better than education, more powerful than psychology and easier to understand than neuroscience . . . this is a paradigm shift in our understanding of the teaching profession" (p. 1). In the succeeding chapters, the following superpowers will be revealed.

Superpower #1 *Introducing Your Superpowered Brain*: *Knowing How It Works* outlines the book's thesis that new neurosciences advances have uncovered "superpowers" readily available to all teachers through a clearer understanding of the science of learning and brain-informed teaching methods.

Superpower #2 *Fueling the Neurobiology of Attention and Engagement* will examine the human brain's remarkable interplay of attention and engagement and how they are powerfully connected to student learning. Highlighted will be ways teachers may create conditions that increase student motivation by tapping into brain factors that affect attention and engagement.

Superpower #3 *Engaging Emotions and Mindsets: Two Potent Forces* will discuss the critical role of emotions in cognition by addressing two aspects: (1) why it is essential for teachers to understand the central role of emotion in cognitive processes and (2) how growth mindset theory is rooted in neuroscience through the construct of brain plasticity.

Superpower #4 *Collaboration: The Brain-to-Brain Learning Boost* will demonstrate how neuroscience explains how student-to-student collaboration boosts the teaching–learning equation.

Superpower #5 *Making It Sticky: Boosting Long-Term Memory* will focus on the neurobiological factors of long-term memory storage.

Superpower #6 *Transformative Questioning* will transform practices related to traditional classroom questioning into ones for which all students may reap both the learning and the social benefits making it a virtual superpower.

Superpower #7 *Transforming Assessments Into Learning Opportunities (LOPPS)* will explore the changing landscape of assessments, including the potency of renaming summative assessments as *learning opportunities*, the power of formative assessments, and the untapped learning potential of student self-assessment.

Superpower #8 *Sparking the Brain's Creative Forces* will demonstrate to teachers how the pedagogies of service-learning and changemaking will invite teachers to consider a broader view of creativity beyond the arts, including decision-making, problem-solving, and design-thinking.

Superpower #9 *Promoting Culturally Responsive and Relevant Teaching* will address the brain principles underlying why culturally responsive/culturally sustaining teaching is effective and its critical importance in meeting the needs of our growing culturally, racially, ethnically, and linguistically diverse student body.

Superpower #10 *Championing Neurodiversity: Valuing the SMART in Every Student* will explain how teachers may embrace neurodiversity and even convert it into a superpower by diversifying ways for learners to receive information, process it, and demonstrate their understanding.

And, if you will pardon one additional reference to Superman . . . Up, up, and away!

REFERENCES

Tokuhama-Espinosa, T. (2011). Why mind, brain, and education sciences is the "new" brain-based education. *New Horizons for Learning*, *9*(1).

Whitman, G., & Kellaher, I. (2016). *Neuro-teach: Brain science and the future of education*. Roman & Littlefield.

NOTES

WHAT MAKES KNOWING ABOUT THE BRAIN A SUPERPOWER?

The role of neuroscience in education not only transforms the practices that take place in the classroom, but it is also empowering for the teacher—equipping them with the tools they need to feel successful in their work.

–Teacher, Sixth grade

I love what we have been learning about the brain. It is changing my day-to-day teaching. Now, I feel that it also makes sense for my students to understand as well so that they will understand the amazing power of their brain.

–Teacher, Third grade

After completing this course, I believe that every educator should be required to have the foundations of the workings of the brain so that we can serve our students at an optimal level.

–Teacher, High school

I chose to open the first chapter with quotes from teachers who, after taking my graduate course on educational neuroscience, experienced a transformative "aha" moment. They came to understand why knowing how the brain works is critical for teachers. After all, we engage with students' brains every single day. They also concluded that this information may be equally valuable for students as they begin to grasp the incredible learning power of their own brains.

Chapter 1 invites you to activate one of your most effective superpowers—teaching in ways that optimize how your students' brains take in, process, and store information. Let us begin with a brief discussion of educational neuroscience.

WHAT IS EDUCATIONAL NEUROSCIENCE?

Educational neuroscience is a burgeoning field connecting science, psychology, and education. Bruer (2016) defines it this way, "Educational neuroscience is a relatively new and highly interdisciplinary field of study. Its objective is to improve educational practice by applying findings from brain research" (p. 1). Moreover, interest in the brain is not just a new phenomenon. As far back as antiquity, scientists and philosophers inquired about the workings of the human brain. As Neil deGrasse Tyson, the renowned cosmologist, eloquently remarked, "Everything we do, every thought we've ever had, is produced by the human brain. But exactly how it operates remains one of the biggest unsolved mysteries, and it seems the more we probe its secrets, the more surprises we find" (n.d.).

Still, it has only been until recently that the brain has given up some of its deepest secrets. In the 1990s, scientists uncovered more knowledge about the brain than in all the previous centuries combined. This leap in understanding was made possible by ever-growing advances in medical technologies that include magnetic resonance imaging (MRI), computerized axial tomography (CAT scans), and positron emission tomography (PET scans) (Hansen et al., 2015). As a result of these advances, the United States declared the 1990s the "decade of the brain" (Friler & Stabio, 2018).

The following contributions were derived from these three decades of research:

- the creation of educational neuroscience as an interdisciplinary field of studies,
- the determination of how neuroscience may be of benefit to educators at all levels, and
- the translation of sophisticated neuroscience terminology for educators who may not be familiar with the field-specific terminology.

Now, 30 years later, more of these mysteries have slowly been revealed to neuroscientists and have informed medicine, mental health, and, more recently, education. Although the practical uses of neuroscience have taken longer to influence educational practices, the field of educational neuroscience was launched. Furthermore, the classroom practices that have emerged from this new field have become known variously as brain-based learning (Caine & Caine, 1997); mind, brain, education (MBE) (Tokuhama-Espinosa, 2010); brain-targeted teaching (Hardiman et al., 2012); and brain-informed teaching (Whitman & Kellaher, 2016). In this book, the term *brain-centered instruction* will be used to describe teaching practices centered on the science of learning (SoL) emerging from the educational neurosciences. In the remaining chapters, I intend to make the case that using these brain-centered instructional practices is akin to having teaching superpowers and may even assist you in *leaping over tall standards in a single bound.*

However, before we move into the heart of the book's thesis, I must also add one important caveat. Educational neuroscience is not meant to be prescriptive regarding specific instructional strategies. Rather, this information may be useful as a basis for informed decision-making to augment your own understanding of effective instruction.

Education Has Been Slow to Embrace Neuroscience

Even after the 1990s breakthrough discoveries from the "decade of the brain," the field of education has not placed educational neuroscience at the forefront of teacher professional development. True, there has been a major movement in the past decade toward understanding the science of learning (SoL). The Deans for Impact (2015) publication defines SoL this way: "*The Science of Learning* summarizes existing cognitive-science research on how students learn and connects it to practical implications for teaching" (p. 2).

The science of learning has roots in three substantial research bases:

1. The seminal publication *How People Learn: Brain, Mind, Experience, and School* (Bransford et al., 1999) significantly impacted the field of education by examining countless research studies and identifying three principles key to learning:

    i.   engagement of learners' prior understandings and experiences,

    ii. building students' conceptual frameworks, and

    iii. assisting learners to monitor their own thinking-metacognition.

2. The passage of the No Child Left Behind (NCLB) Act in 2001 spawned countless research investigations in the United States with a goal to identify educational practices *proven effective through rigorous scientific research*, a provision of the legislation. Based on the meta-analyses of hundreds of former studies, the Mid-Continent Research for Education and Learning (McREL) isolated nine categories of instructional strategies that are most likely to improve student achievement. These findings were published in the groundbreaking book *Classroom Instruction That Works* (Marzano et al., 2001) and contained the following evidence-based teaching practices:

    *   *Identifying similarities and differences:* how items, events, processes, or concepts are similar and different based on characteristics

    *   *Summarizing and note-taking:* identifying what is most important about the learning and restating that knowledge in their own words

- *Reinforcing effort and providing recognition:* taking note of the effort the student has made and acknowledging that accomplishment for a student
- *Homework and practice:* providing students with opportunities to deepen understanding of content and skills through continued practice
- *Nonlinguistic representations:* visual, tactile, and kinesthetic modes of learning
- *Cooperative learning:* the ability to learn and work in groups
- *Setting objectives and providing feedback:* creating learning targets and giving feedback that is timely and specific
- *Generating and testing hypotheses:* creating and testing possible claims and providing evidence for those claims
- *Cues, questions, and advance organizers:* providing students with a structured framework to process new content

3. In the book *Visible Learning* (2008), Hattie, the director of the Melbourne Education Research Institute at the University of Melbourne, Australia, investigated an astonishing number of different studies—146,142 to be exact—searching for attributes positively associated with student learning. He termed these *high-impact teaching practices.* Many districts are currently basing their professional development on these identified instructional practices.

Perhaps now is the time to add findings from educational neuroscience to the current research on the science of learning (SoL). The wider understanding of the phenomenon of neuroplasticity (i.e., the ability of the brain to continue to grow connections throughout life) has created an opening to fully embrace this newer science that may change the way educators teach and are trained. Neuroscience maintains that all people can learn to high levels due to *brain plasticity*, or the brain's ability to grow via dendritic branching.

 ## WHAT MAKES KNOWING ABOUT THE BRAIN A SUPERPOWER? EXAMINING THE RESEARCH

Let us start with the basics. "Learning is innately linked to the biological and chemical forces that control the human brain" (Hileman, 2006, p. 18). Furthermore, every brain, and I do mean *every* brain, has an unfathomable number of brain cells, or neurons, that aid learning. The number has been calculated at approximately 100 billion (Azevedo et al., 2009). However, that is only the tip of the iceberg. Each neuron has the ability to connect with other brain cells (some say between 1,000 and 100,000), which makes the number of possible connections in the brain astronomical. As Wilson and Conyers (2020) remarked, "Potentially, a single cubic centimeter of cortex may have as many connections as there are stars in the Milky Way galaxy" (p. 33). The incomprehensibly large number of possible connections in every human brain gives new meaning to the oft-uttered phrase "All students can learn."

NEURO-LINK: Teacher expectations affect student learning (Brophy, 1983; Brophy & Good, 1974; Rosenthal & Jacobson, 1968).

Decades before the term *educational neuroscience* was even uttered, evidence for the power of teacher expectations was made abundantly clear. One study was quite well known. Indeed, it shook up the entire educational world. Published in 1968 by Rosenthal and Jacobson, the findings provide irrefutable evidence that teacher expectations could significantly affect student achievement. In this study, researchers told teachers that two students (in each of their classrooms) were primed to make rapid intellectual growth based on recent I.Q. testing of the entire class. This assertion was untrue, as the two named students in each class were chosen at random. However, by the end of the year, the students the teachers *expected* to perform well showed significantly higher gains in intellectual growth than their classmates. The only factor that could have accounted for this level of growth would have been the way the teachers *treated* these pre-identified (and randomly selected) students. In large and small ways, teachers communicated to them how smart they were! Over the years, many subsequent studies have widely supported the general findings of the original 1968 study and, together, have become known as the Pygmalion effect. (Note other examples of the Pygmalion effect on this website: https://bit.ly/3spydR0.) As I stated in the previous paragraph, your grasping of the sheer number of neurons in each of your student's brains can become a superpower—maybe even your most potent superpower—as it taps into this compelling accumulation of data on the power of teacher expectations and the principles of neuroplasticity.

NEURO-LINK: Teachers who incorporate more of these brain-centered teaching practices into their instructional repertoire create more impactful lessons (Dubinsky et al., 2013; Hardiman et al., 2012; Mayer, 2017; Tan & Amiel, 2022).

From understanding concepts of neuroplasticity (foundational to growth mindset theory) to creating spaced practice opportunities for students, to the tenets of attention and motivation, the numerous findings from neuroscience can help shape student learning. And there is more. According to Hardiman et al. (2012), "Educators now have relevant information about the neural and cognitive underpinnings of emotion, which affects learning in important ways via its influence on higher cognitive functions" (p. 136). Dubinsky et al. (2013) agree that "neuroscience concepts can be used to *directly* improve teachers' understanding of student learning and development" (p. 327).

Principles of Brain-Centered Instruction

In 1990, at the beginning of the decade of the brain, Caine and Caine identified principles of how the brain works and refined these ideas in 1990 and 1994. Applied to education, they called these the "12 principles of brain-based learning." These tenets are still being referenced worldwide in books, articles, and educational programs today. I have chosen five of these with which to frame this book. In each succeeding chapter, practical classroom ideas will be presented to connect these principles with newer research in educational neuroscience to empower your classroom instruction.

 Principle #1 The brain/mind is social.

Human beings are social animals. According to Gopnik et al. (1999), all humans have the "contact urge." Moreover, recent research has just confirmed that this social nature of human beings is grounded in biology through the scientific explorations of mirror neurons. *Mirror neurons* are networks of pairs of neurons that will fire when a person acts or when that person observes the same action performed by someone else, mimicking the actions of the one being observed (Lacoboni et al., 2005).

 Principle #2 The search for meaning is innate.

Humans have a biological imperative to make sense of things. This tendency has been called the *explanatory drive* (Gopnik et al., 1999). Each person's brain must process enormous amounts of incoming sensory information in a single day. To deal with this task, the brain has set up filtering systems to weed out nonessential information. The most essential information (meaningful) gets the attention of the brain. And conversely, the brain resists isolated bits of information perceived as meaningless.

 Principle #3 The search for meaning occurs through patterning.

One of the main tasks of the brain is to perceive patterns (Restak, 1995). Cognitive scientists have created many terms to describe patterning, such as categories, frames, and schemata. Patterning is accomplished when the brain categorizes information into a larger schema called programs. A corollary to this principle is that the brain resists isolated bits of information in favor of these more extensive patterned programs where everything is connected.

 Principle #4 Emotions are critical to learning.

Neuroscientists are beginning to understand emotions' significant role in learning (Pert, 1997). Damasio (1999) confirmed that new dendritic connections are created when learning occurs. What was not previously known is that these connections also include the learner's emotions. Moreover, these emotions may be connected to the learning for life or until another emotionally powerful experience replaces the original learning.

 Principle #5 Each brain is uniquely organized.

The dendritic branching of our brains is like no other human on the planet because no other person has had the exact experiences we have had. This fact creates a paradox as every human is similar to and different from all others.

Two decades after the Caines' founding brain principles, Crossland (2010) offered the following eight messages for teachers to consider. I have added corollaries to Crossland's original ideas.

- The brain is built to learn. *Each student has the cognitive hardware to learn.*

- All learning has an emotional component. *Emotions are not secondary to learning; they are an essential component.*

- The brain is not fixed and has the capacity to adapt. *Plasticity is a foundational force for each brain.*

- Maturation occurs at different rates for different individuals. *Differentiation is not a deficit. It is built into our brains from birth.*

- The transfer of information in the brain is both electrical and chemical. *The speed of thought in our brain is faster than that of light and still somewhat of a mystery.*

- Forgetting is a sign of a healthy brain. *Errors and mistakes have an essential role in learning.*

- Supportive teaching using scaffolding and feedback is essential. *New connections in the brain form more efficiently when the learner's mistakes can be corrected during the misunderstanding.*

- Collaborating is essential for learning. *Peer-to-peer collaboration creates additional channels for storing information.*

CLAIMING YOUR BRAIN–CENTERED SUPERPOWERS

Playful as the title of this book may be, the message for educators is genuine. In the pages of the coming chapters, you will be invited to consider implications for your classroom instruction stemming from evolving research in the educational neurosciences.

 ## USING THIS SUPERPOWER IN YOUR CLASSROOM: TEACHING YOUR STUDENTS ABOUT THEIR BRAIN

I will now return to the claim made at the beginning of the chapter; that is, knowing about the brain is not enough. Your most effective superpower exists in teaching your students about the incredible learning power of their own brains. Quite simply, this information has the potential to amplify attention, motivation, engagement, emotional connections, and memory retention.

Let us begin with a "shout-out" to a VST, a very special teacher. As a board-certified neurologist and leading authority in educational neuroscience, Dr. Judy Willis chose to go back to school to earn her teaching license to discover first-hand how these principles of brain-centered teaching would/could be applied to everyday classroom instruction. A strong advocate for teaching students how their brain operates, she observed, "When I began incorporating basic instruction about the brain into my classes and teaching simple activities to improve brain processing, students not only became more engaged and confident, but they also began changing their study practices in ways that paid off in higher achievement" (Willis, 2009/2010, para. 3).

Other researchers have also advocated for students to learn about their brains (Gage, 2019). Moreover, in response to this call, countless secondary schools have added neuroscience courses to the curriculum. These courses are steps in the right direction. However, all students should learn about the wonders of their own brains, not just those in science classes.

Brain 101 for Students (and Their Teachers)

A beginning lesson on the brain may be the first step. These suggestions would be adjusted for students' ages and developmental levels.

- **Brain parts:** Have students make fists and put their fists together, knuckles to knuckles, forming a hands-on (forgive the pun) model of the two hemispheres of the brain. Explain that this is a model of their brain and within these two parts lies billions of neurons, or brain cells.

- **Number of neurons (brain cells) in every brain:**
  - » Either digitally (Google Slides) or on the board, create a multiple-choice quiz to ask: How many neurons do humans have in their brain?

    A. 1,000, B. 1 million, C. 1 billion, D. 100+ billion

    (Answer D. 100+ billion)
  - » To give students an idea of how large a number that is, have older students try to calculate how much time it would take to count to 1 billion, if they counted one number every second (no sleeping or eating). (Answer: 31 years, 251 days, 6 hours, 50 minutes, 46 seconds)

- **Neuroplasticity: How the Brain Can Grow New Dendrites**
  - » Teaching your students about neuroplasticity—the idea that each brain is, in a way, plastic and constantly grows new dendrites as learning happens—is one of the best and most hopeful gifts you can give them.
  - » Growth mindset theory is based entirely on the premise of neuroplasticity. Carol Dweck (2014) explains that a growth mindset is understanding that skills and abilities can grow and change over time due to the ability of dendrites to grow in the brain. Dweck also shares the power of the word *yet* and how that single word helps students understand there is potential for growth (and getting smarter). Teachers who add the powerful two words *not yet* gift their students with the belief that they will eventually be successful in their learning pursuit (Dweck, 2014).
  - » With this knowledge, they can begin to form a growth mindset, knowing that intelligence can be developed versus the idea that it is set in stone and static, which is called a "fixed mindset."
  - » Study after study points to growth mindset being key to students' believing that effort matters and that they CAN learn.
  - » The act of getting something wrong is a key part of learning, prompting rewiring of the brain as the student works to get it right (TED, 2016).

- **Making Friends With Your Amygdala**
  - » Let students know that emotions and learning go hand in hand.
  - » Have them close their eyes and think of a time when they felt unmotivated to learn. Ask, "What assignment were you doing?" "What were you thinking about?" "Were you stressed?" "Bored?"

» Display a picture of the amygdala, and explain that the emotional hub of our brain is our amygdala. When we are stressed or feeling bored, the amygdala moves us into one of these states—flight, fight, or freeze—and will not allow information to get to the thinking part of our brain. In a state of boredom, the "flight" means we start to daydream. However, being absorbed in an interesting challenge helps the amygdala stay engaged because we are less likely to be bored or uninterested.

» When we are interested and feel calm, our amygdala allows information to enter our thinking brain, helping us learn.

» Tell students that when they enter the classroom, they are in a safe space, and you will do your part to make learning interesting, giving them some choice, and keeping the environment calm and focused. They can use visualizations of a calm place and deep breathing to stay calm.

- **Superpowered Memory Techniques**

   » Show students a picture of the hippocampus, or memory center, in the brain.

   » Tell them that for something to be stored there, there must be strong neural (dendrite-to-dendrite) connections. Explain that myelin is created when they practice and try to recall, or remember, information. Neural pathways that are not used fade away.

   » Consult Chapter 5 for ideas of ways to help students' long-term retention of information.

SUPERPOWERED RESOURCES

Due to the current interest in the role of neuroscience in everyday classroom instruction, the internet is virtually overflowing with resources about the brain. The following materials have been assembled to support your ongoing professional learning in this field and to promote the argument that brain-centered instruction may empower student learning at all levels.

 **Websites**

- Resources on Learning and the Brain

  https://bit.ly/467AFt6

This collection on the main Edutopia website hosts articles, videos, and other links for exploring the connection between education and neuroscience.

- Brain-Based Learning

http://www.brainbasedlearning.net

Teachers will find many articles and classroom resources to teach with an understanding of how the brain works.

- Neuroscience for Kids

https://bit.ly/46dBWyA

A monthly newsletter offered by Eric Chudler, Ph.D., a neuroscientist and executive director of the Center for Neurotechnology in Seattle, Washington

 Videos

- **The Mysterious Workings of the Adolescent Brain**

https://bit.ly/3SFadDX

- **Growing Evidence of Brain Plasticity**

https://bit.ly/46e2tfe

- **How We Learn**

https://bit.ly/479MCQp

- **How to Learn Math for Teachers and Parents: Brain Plasticity**

https://bit.ly/3MEFJOw

Books/Articles

Children's Literature

- Deak, J. (2010). *Your fantastic elastic brain: A growth mindset book for kids to stretch and shape their brains*. Little Pickle Press.

- Nguyen, B., & Pham, B. (2022). *Neurology for kids: A fun picture book about the nervous system for children*. Black Phoenix Press.

- Seluk, N. (2019). *The brain is kind of a big deal*. Orchard Books.

- Sooful, P. (2023). *My brain is magic: A sensory-seeking celebration*. Soaring Kite Books.

Adult Literature

- Heller, R. (2018). What we know (and think we know) about the learning brain: An interview with Tracey Tokuhama-Espinosa. *Phi Delta Kappan, 100*(4), 24–30.

- Immordino-Yang, M. H., & Damasio, A. (2007). We feel, therefore we learn: The relevance of affective and social neuroscience to education. *Mind, Brain, and Education, 1*(1), 3–10.

- Jensen, E., & Snider, C. (2013). *Turnaround tools for the teenage brain: Helping underperforming students become lifelong learners*. Jossey-Bass.

- Sousa, D., & Tomlinson, C. (2011). *Differentiation and the brain: How neuroscience supports the learner-friendly classroom*. Solution Tree.

- Sprenger, M. (2018). *How to teach so students remember* (2nd ed.). ASCD.

- Whitman, G., & Kellaher, I. (2016). *Neuro-teach: Brain science and the future of education*. Rowman & Littlefield.

- Wolfe, P. (2010). *Brain matters: Translating research into classroom practice* (2nd ed.). ASCD.

REFERENCES

Azevedo, F. A. C., Carvalho, L. R. B., Grinberg, L. T., Farfel, J. M., Ferretti, R. E. L., Leite, R. E. P., Jacob, F. W., Lent, R., & Herculano-Houzel, S. (2009). Equal numbers of neuronal and non-neuronal cells make the human brain an isometrically scaled-up primate brain. *Journal of Comparative Neurology, 513*, 532–541.

Bransford, J. D., Brown, A. L., & Cocking, R. R. (Eds.). (1999). *How people learn: Brain, mind, experience, and school*. National Academies Press.

Brophy, J. (1983). Research on the self-fulfilling prophecy and teacher expectations, *Journal of Educational Psychology*, *75*(5), 631–661.

Brophy, J., & Good, T. (1974). *Teacher-student relationships: Causes and consequences*. Holt.

Bruer, J. T. (2016). Where is educational neuroscience? *Educational Neuroscience*, *1*, 1–12.

Caine, G., & Caine, R. N. (1997). *Education on the edge of possibility*. ASCD.

Caine, R. N., & Caine, G. (1990). Understanding a brain-based approach to learning and teaching. *Educational Leadership*, *48*(2), 66–70.

Caine, R. N., & Caine, G. (1994). *Making connections: Teaching and the human brain*. Addison-Wesley.

Crossland, J. (2010). Brain biology and learning. *School Science Review*, *91*(337), 99–107.

Damasio, A. (1999). *The feeling of what happens: Body and emotion in the making of consciousness*. Harcourt College.

Deans for Impact. (2015). *The science of learning*.

Dubinsky, J. M., Roehrig, G., & Varma, S. (2013). Infusing neuroscience into teacher professional development. *Educational Researcher*, *42*(6), 317–329. https://doi.org/10.3102/0013189X13499403

Dweck, C. (2014). Teachers' mindsets: "Every student has something to teach me." *Educational Horizons*, *93*(2), 10–15.

Friler, J. B., & Stabio, M. E. (2018). Three pillars of educational neuroscience from three decades of literature. *Trends in Neuroscience and Education*, *13*, 17–25.

Gage, G. (2019). The case for neuroscience research in the classroom. *Neuron*, *102*(5), 914–917. https://doi.org/10.1016/j.neuron.2019.04.007

Gopnik, A., Meltzoff, A., & Kuhl, P. K. (1999). *The scientist in the crib: Minds, brains, and how children learn*. William Morrow.

Hansen, B., Buczynski, S., & Puckett, K. (2015). *Curriculum and teaching for the 21st century*. Bridgepoint Education.

Hardiman, M., Rinne, L., Gregory, E., & Yarmolinskaya, J. (2012). Neuroethics, neuroeducation, and classroom teaching: Where the brain sciences meet pedagogy. *Neuroethics*, *5*, 135–143. https://doi.org/10.1007/s12152-011-9116-6

Hattie, J. (2008). *Visible learning*. Routledge.

Hileman, S. (2006). Motivating students using brain-based teaching strategies. *The Agricultural Education Magazine*, *78*(4), 18–20.

Immordino-Yang, M. H., & Damasio, A. (2007). We feel, therefore we learn: The relevance of affective and social neuroscience to education. Mind, Brain, and Education, *1(1), 3–10*.

Lacoboni, M., Molnar-Szakacs, I., Gallese, V., Buccino, G., Mazziotta, J. C., & Rizzolatti, G. (2005). Grasping the intentions of others with one's own mirror neuron system. *PLoS Biology*, *3*(3), e79. https://doi.org/10.1371/journal.pbio.0030079

Marzano, R. J., Pickering, D. J., & Pollock, J. E. (2001). *Classroom instruction that works: Research-based strategies for increasing student achievement.* Association for Supervision and Curriculum Development.

Mayer, R. E. (2017). How can brain research inform academic learning and instruction? *Educational Psychology Review*, *29*(4), 835–846.

Pert, C. B. (1997). *Molecules of emotion*. Scribner.

Restak, R. (1995). *Brainscapes*. Hyperion.

Rosenthal, R., & Jacobson, L. (1968). *Pygmalion in the classroom: Teacher expectation and pupils' intellectual development*. Holt, Rinehart, & Winston.

Tan, Y. S. M., & Amiel, J. J. (2022). Teachers learning to apply neuroscience to classroom instruction: Case of professional development in British Columbia. *Professional Development in Education*, *48*(1), 70–87.

TED. (2016). *Jo Boaler: How you can be good at math, and other surprising facts about learning* [Video]. https://www.youtube.com/watch?v=3icoSeGqQtY

Tokuhama-Espinosa, T. (2010). *The new science of teaching and learning: Using the best of mind, brain, and education science in the classroom*. Teachers College Press.

Tyson, N. D. (n.d.). Quotation. *BrainyQuote*. https://www.brainyquote.com/quotes/neil_de-grasse_tyson_531089#:~:text=Neil%20deGrasse%20Tyson%20Quotes&text=Everything%20we%20do%2C%20every%20thought%20we've%20ever%20had%2C,the%20more%20surprises%20we%20find

Whitman, G., & Kellaher, I. (2016). *Neuro-teach: Brain science and the future of education*. Roman & Littlefield.

Willis, J. (December 2009/January 2010). *How to teach students about the brain*. Association for Supervision and Curriculum Development. http://www.ascd.org/publications/educational-leadership/dec09/vol67/num04/How-to-Teach-Students-About-the-Brain.aspx

Wilson, D. L., & Conyers, M. A. (2020). *Developing growth mindsets: Principles and practices for maximizing students' potential*. Association for Supervision and Curriculum Development.

FUELING THE NEUROBIOLOGY OF ATTENTION AND ENGAGEMENT

The more teachers talk during a lesson, the less time there is for student engagement.

–Sousa and Toth (2020)

Attention is thought to be the gateway between information and learning.

–Keller et al. (2020)

A computer game doesn't hand out cash, toys, or even hugs. The motivation to persevere is the brain seeking another surge of dopamine—the fuel of intrinsic reinforcement.

–Judy Willis (2011)

Chapter 2 will examine the remarkable interplay of attention and engagement in the human brain and how they are powerfully connected to student learning. Highlighted will be ways teachers may create conditions that increase student motivation by tapping into brain factors that affect attention and engagement. Specific pedagogies such as inquiry-based teaching will be showcased as the brain fires on all cylinders when it has a problem to solve, making it a super-superpower.

WHAT MAKES ATTENTION AND ENGAGEMENT SUPERPOWERS: EXAMINING THE RESEARCH

Pay attention! Teachers everywhere have uttered those two words countless times in their classrooms, all without fully understanding the intricacies of the phenomenon we call "paying attention." In neuroscience, *attention* is defined as the "brain's ability to concentrate on only one thing at a time" (Hovington et al., 2015, p. 47). Let us examine a few crucial findings from neuroscience that address this critical element.

 NEURO-LINK: The brain automatically controls attention (Sousa, 2011).

Many occurrences happen in our brain between the first sensory arousal and long-term memory. Sousa describes this sequence as having four stages. The first stage lasts only a few seconds and occurs when we notice information from one of our five senses. It should be noted that at this stage, our brain discards most of the incoming information as it is deemed nonessential. Neuroscientists have shed some light on why this dumping happens. Incoming information to the brain can come as fast as 11 million bits per second, but we can only process about 120 bits per second (Levitin & Menon, 2005). Therefore, the math confirms that most of what comes in goes right out again.

Now that we have the brain's attention, several more critical components must happen before learning occurs. Information that makes it through the first stage moves to *immediate memory*, lasting only about 30 seconds. If we deem the information important enough, it moves to the third stage, working memory, where it can be held for about 5–20 minutes. The information is gone if we do not engage with it at that point. Goodwin (2018) uses this amusing analogy to describe what happens next: "Whether information completes the final stage of the journey and finds a home in long-term memory depends on whether we decide to go on more than one date, so to speak, with the new information through further repetition, rehearsal, contextualization, or application" (p. 4). As you may surmise, due to the enormous amounts of new information flowing through our brain daily, most of it is discarded during stages 1 through 3 (Figure 2.1).

Figure 2.1   Brain Stages: Memory Storage

Stage 1 Senses are aroused → Stage 2 Immediate memory 30 seconds → Stage 3 Working memory 5–20 minutes → Stage 4 Long-term memory

Source: Adapted from Goodwin (2018).

The goal for teachers is to intentionally supercharge engagement opportunities for learners that may work to thwart the natural brain's function of forgetting. The following section will provide a CUE for you to accomplish this goal.

Implications for Teaching: A CUE for You

As we have seen, engagement is everything. Magic happens if a student is engaged in a lesson or can connect with a topic. This statement seems obvious, but it holds added power because it is backed by neuroscience. When we design our lessons so that students perceive they has relevance for them or they can connect with them emotionally, engagement and thus learning are enhanced (Whitman & Kelleher, 2016, p. 89). Employing CUE (Hansen et al., 2015) can expedite student engagement. CUE stands for creative, useful, and emotional. Let us explore each of these.

Creative

The brain is hardwired to notice novel stimuli (Chen et al., 2020). This information is not unfamiliar to teachers who have long known that creative lessons attract students' attention. What may be new is what the brain does when presented with novelty. According to Le Doux (2003), specific neurotransmitters are released that make it nearly impossible for a person not to pay attention. As mentioned earlier in the chapter, the brain lights up everywhere to understand the novel stimulus.

Useful

Researchers (Gu et al., 2021) assert that the most powerful way to attract the brain's attention and convince it to engage is for incoming information to be perceived by the learner as being useful or relevant. Notice that the phrase "to be perceived by the learner" is critical as almost all information is relevant to the teacher. How may this be accomplished? Providing choices during the school day is one easy way teachers may create opportunities for students to find personal meaning within the curriculum (Patall et al., 2010). What is more exciting is that brain scans (fMRI) revealed increased arousal and attentional processing when test subjects were given choices in their tasks (Han, 2021). (The following section will examine various ways choice may be inserted easily into most lessons.)

Purpose is another potent motivator for students. Caram and Davis (2005/2019) maintain that students engage in lessons they view as purposeful and that "creating a culture of investigation is a key component" (p. 20). I want to close with a comment from a middle school teacher that perfectly sums up this idea, "Not every single one of my lessons has to be meaningful, but I want to find more moments of learning in each day for which students will find purpose and personal meaning."

Emotional

An axiom in learning theory is that emotion drives attention, and attention drives memory, learning, problem-solving, and behavior (Sylwester, 2003). In other words, we must pay attention to what we need to learn. Moreover, according to neuroscience, humans are more likely to pay attention if emotions are activated. Sousa (2009) explains the phenomenon like this:

> *When people feel positive about a learning situation, chemicals called endorphins and dopamine become active. Endorphins provide a feeling of euphoria. Dopamine stimulates the prefrontal cortex, keeping the individual attentive, interactive, and likely to remember what he or she experiences. Negative feelings, on the other hand, cause the hormone cortisol to enter the bloodstream. Cortisol puts the brain into survival mode; this shifts the brain's attention away from learning so it can deal with the source of stress. Instead of learning, the brain remembers the pressure and registers these kinds of situations as unpleasant. (p. 1)*

A key challenge for teachers remains how to sustain students' attention and engagement in every subject all year long. This feat is an art form and not easily accomplished. Adding to this challenge is the reality that engagement is constantly in flux. Nevertheless, Sousa and Toth (2020) assert that student engagement is a necessary condition for deep learning and that it would be wise for teachers to understand engagement from a neurocognitive perspective. They share this reminder, "We know that the more students engage and probe the learning, look for other applications, and discuss alternative solutions, the greater the number of neural pathways that are activated in their brains" (para. 3).

As discussed earlier in the chapter, each brain continuously monitors sensory input to decide what will be allowed to move forward and what will be discarded. This *sorting system* is highly subjective to each individual's needs. A key criterion rests on the question, "Is this information *important* to me *right now*?" Incoming data deemed to have *relevancy* is noticed by the brain immediately. There is one important caveat. The relevancy, or meaningfulness, must be for the learner and not just the teacher. Experiential learning has a greater possibility of being seen as meaningful to learners.

USING THIS SUPERPOWER IN YOUR CLASSROOM

I have long envied conductors who, at the swipe of a wand, have the complete attention of 100% of the members of the orchestra. Although we classroom teachers never achieve this feat, let us examine some powerful concepts from neuroscience that teachers may employ to engage most of our students most of the time.

Dewey (1938) is most credited with the theory of learning by doing, or experiential learning, which rests on three constructs: (1) People learn best when they are personally involved in the learning experience, (2) knowledge has to be discovered by the individual if it is to have any significant meaning to them or make a difference in their behavior, and (3) a person's commitment to learning is highest when they have some element of choice or freedom to set their own learning pathways within a specific framework (Dewey, 1938, as cited in Smith, 1980, p. 16). Following are four different teaching structures that are experiential and inspire and animate personal meaning and choice.

Inquiry-Based Learning

Inquiry-based learning creates instant engagement for students by asking them to generate questions that will guide them in actively exploring a topic. Following are some inquiry questions that support student engagement in science, mathematics, social students, and language arts.

Science

- *How do trees help the environment?*
- *What are some ways humans can lower their carbon footprint?*
- *How do animals help humans?*
- *What are some consequences when the rainforest is destroyed?*
- *How do electric cars help the environment?*
- *In what ways may AI be helpful? Harmful?*

Social Studies

- *How do community workers help us?*
- *What cultural event(s) may have shaped your family?*
- *What can be learned from historical photos?*
- *What are ways that Google Earth can be used to help humans?*

- *Identify a U.S. president and provide evidence for the good things he accomplished.*
- *What can we learn from explorers?*
- *Why is it important to study history?*
- *How do museums help us understand the story of human civilization?*

Math

- *What are several ways that math makes life easier for people? Explain.*
- *What occupations use math the most?*
- *What geometric shapes are found in the natural world?*
- *How can we use graphs to help us understand the relationship between population and pollution?*
- *Explore the patterns and relationships between addition, subtraction, multiplication, and division.*

Language Arts

- *Investigate different genres of literature. What kinds are most popular?*
- *Explore all the ways that ancient peoples communicated with one another.*
- *What is the role of the press in a democracy?*
- *What are some famous speeches that have present-day relevance?*
- *What would you include if you were to send a communication to outer space to describe our life on Earth?*

Game-Based Learning

If you have been teaching longer than a week, you most certainly have discovered the superpowered benefits of adding games to your classroom routines. Game-based learning allows for enhanced student engagement, motivation, and opportunities for structured social interaction in classrooms from early primary grades through high school. Some genres of games include the following:

- TV game shows (Jeopardy, Concentration, Who Wants to Be a Millionaire?)
- Professional sports (baseball, football, basketball, soccer)
- Bingo-like games that use the familiar game of BINGO in the learning of content
- Teacher-created (e.g., Teachers Pay Teachers)

- Student-created (Students create board games based on content areas of math, social studies, science, and literacy)
- Commercial games (Scrabble, Battleship, Mastermind)
- Digital games (coding, science simulations in game format, math games, literature genres, historical games)

SUPERPOWERED RESOURCES

Here are some additional resources (websites, videos, and books/articles) for engaging students.

 Websites

- Learning by Inquiry

https://www.learningbyinquiry.com/

This site has many resources for TK–12 teachers, especially inquiry questions for students.

- High Tech High

https://bit.ly/3QEFBQp

High Tech High is a Charter School organization that employs project-based learning in Grades K–12.

Videos

- *Judy Willis on the Science of Learning: Big Thinkers*

https://bit.ly/3FYa07j

- What Is Inquiry-Based Learning?

https://bit.ly/3SNeHbA

This engaging YouTube video uses clips from the Harry Potter movies to explain inquiry learning.

Books/Articles

- **Game-Based Learning**

https://bit.ly/46dRFh9

- **What the Heck Is Inquiry-Based Learning?**

https://bit.ly/3sxnTWX

- **What Is Inquiry-Based Learning?**

https://bit.ly/3SC6zed

REFERENCES

Blondal, K. S., & Adalbjarnardottir, S. (2012). Student disengagement in relation to expected and unexpected educational pathways. *Scandinavian Journal of Educational Research*, *56*, 85–100.

Caram, C. A., & Davis, P. B. (2019). Inviting student engagement with questioning. In C. Abla & B. R. Fraumeni (Eds.), *Student engagement: Evidence-based strategies to boost academic and social-emotional results*. McREL International. (Reprinted from "Inviting student engagement with questioning," 2005, Fall, *Kappa Delta Pi Record*, 19–23)

Chen, S., He, L., Huang, A. J. Y., Boehringer, R., Robert, V., Wintzer, M. E., Polygalov, D., Weitemier, A. Z., Tao, Y., Gu, M., Middleton, S. J., Namiki, K., Hama, H., Therreau, L., Chevaleyre, V., Hioki, H., Miyawaki, A., Piskorowski, R. A., & McHugh, T. J. (2020). A hypo-thalamic novelty signal modulates hippocampal memory. *Nature*, *586*(7828), 270–274. https://doi.org/10.1038/s41586-020-2771-1

Dewey, J. (1938). *Experience and education*. Macmillan Company.

Evanovich, L., Harbour, K., Hughes, L., & Sweigart, C. (2015). A brief review of effective teaching practices that maximize student engagement. *Preventing School Failure*, *59*(1), 5–13. https://doi.org/10.1080/1045988X.2014.919136

Goodwin, B. (2018). *Student learning that works: How brain science informs a student learning model.* McREL International.

Gu, Q., Lam, N. H., Wimmer, R. D., Halassa, M. M., & Murray, J. D. (2021). *Computational circuit mechanisms underlying thalamic control of attention.* BioRxiv. https://www.biorxiv.org/content/10.1101/2020.09.16.300749v2

Han, C. (2021). The effects of choice on task performance and reward awareness: A functional magnetic resonance imaging study. *Mind, Brain, and Education*, *15*(4), 299–310. https://doi.org/10.1111/mbe.12299

Hansen, B., Buczynski, S., & Puckett, K. (2015). *Curriculum and teaching for the 21st century.* Bridgepoint Education.

Hovington, C., Ashgar, A., Sharp, S., & Nalbantoglu, J. (2015). How does my brain pay attention? *Science and Children*, *52*(6), 45–53. https://doi.org/10.2505/4/sc150520645

Keller, A. S., Davidesco, I., & Tanner, K. D. (2020). Attention matters: How orchestrating attention may relate to classroom learning. *CBE-Life Sciences Education*, *19*(3), 1–9. https://doi.org/10.1187/cbe.20-05-0106

LeDoux, J. (2003). The emotional brain, fear, and the amygdala. *Cellular and Molecular Neurobiology*, *23*, 727–738. https://doi.org/10.1023/A:1025048802629

Levitin, D. J., & Menon, V. (2005). The neural locus of temporal structure and expectancies in music: Evidence from functional neuroimaging at 3 tesla. *Music Perception*, *22*(3), 563–575. https://doi.org/10.1525/mp.2005.22.3.563

Patall, E. A., Cooper, H., & Wynn, S. R. (2010). The effectiveness and relative importance of choice in the classroom. *Journal of Educational Psychology*, *102*(4), 896–915. https://doi.org/10.1037/a0019545

Smith, M. K. (1980). *Creators not consumers: Rediscovering social education.* Leicester: National Association of Youth Clubs.

Sousa, D. A. (2009, June). Brain-friendly learning for teachers. *Education Leadership*, *66*(9).

Sousa, D. A. (2011). *How the ELL brain learns.* Corwin.

Sousa, D. A., & Toth, M. D. (2020, May). Neuroscience supports successful student academic teams. *ASCD Express*, *15*(18).

Sylwester, R. (2003). *A biological brain in a cultural classroom* (2nd ed.). Corwin.

Tan, K.-L., Lew, T.-Y., & Sim, A. K. S. (2021). Effect of work engagement on meaningful work and psychological capital: Perspectives from social workers in New Zealand. *Employee Relations*, *43*(3), 807–826. https://doi.org/10.1108/ER-11-2019-0433

Whitman, G., & Kelleher, I. (2016). *Neuroteach: Brain science and the future of education.* Rowman & Littlefield.

Willis, J. (2011, April). *A neurologist makes the case for the video game model as a learning tool.* Edutopia. https://www.edutopia.org/blog/neurologist-makes-case-video-game-model-learning-tool

NOTES

ENGAGING EMOTIONS AND MINDSETS:
TWO POTENT FORCES

Emotions are the gateway to cognition and learning.
–Sousa and Tomlinson (2018)

Neuroplasticity is our human superpower.

–Desautels (2023)

The power of yet is not one to be underestimated. It will undoubtedly be the final puzzle piece in making education "the great equalizer" it is meant to be. Its success with historically marginalized students has vast implications.
–Teacher, High school

The advances in educational neuroscience discussed in Chapter 1 have initiated a reexamination of the role of emotions in the learning process. This chapter will discuss the critical role of emotions in cognition by addressing two aspects: (1) why teachers need to understand the central role of emotion in cognitive processes and (2) how growth mindset theory (Dweck, 2014) is rooted in neuroscience through the construct of brain plasticity.

 ## WHAT MAKES EMOTIONS AND MINDSETS SUPERPOWERS? EXAMINING THE RESEARCH

Emotions significantly impact the learning process by enhancing or inhibiting the capacity to absorb and retain information. Motivation and cognition can be enhanced by positive emotions. However, when we are in an anxious or fearful state, learning is inhibited. Where once emotions were called "soft skills" and relegated to lesser importance in classrooms, we now see them being elevated to top-tier status. Let's examine a few important findings that have made this so.

NEURO-LINK: Emotions have a significant influence on cognitive processes (Immordino-Yang & Damasio, 2007; Tyng et al., 2017; Whitman & Kelleher, 2016).

Foundational to the understanding of the impact of emotions on learning there exists a part of the brain to which almost no teacher has paid much attention, the amygdala. Your understanding of this odd-sounding part of the brain could be a potent superpower. Everyone has heard of the fight, flight, or freeze phenomenon. This inborn instinct originates inside a bean-shaped structure in the brain called the *amygdala*. One of the roles of the amygdala is to serve as a watchdog protecting us from harm as it monitors sensory intake and sends it onward to either the thinking part of the brain or to our reactive brain. If all is determined to be safe, the amygdala allows these incoming signals to continue their way to the hippocampus (memory center) and then to higher cortical centers for processing. However, if we are deemed to be in danger, the amygdala immediately readies us for fight, flight, or freeze and prohibits information from proceeding forward.

Neuroscientists have recently learned that stress is perceived by the amygdala in much the same way as a threat. Therefore, when a student is in an anxious state, such as having to work on a math problem in front of the entire class, there is a very real chance that his or her amygdala will prohibit information from advancing to higher brain centers. Given this central role of emotion in cognitive processes (Immordino-Yang & Damasio, 2007), we need to ensure that a positive, safe, and supportive learning environment is available for every student.

 NEURO-LINK: Boredom acts like a stressor on the brain (Tomlinson & Sousa, 2020; Willis, 2021).

Neuroscientists have confirmed that the amygdala reacts to boredom in much the same way as it does when we are anxious or fearful. Let me say that again. *When we are bored, the brain is stressed*. Therefore, while we intend to create these safe environments for our learners, we should also be cognizant of the need to maintain some level of challenge or interest so that the amygdala in each student's brain will allow new information to be forwarded to higher cortical processing centers. Researchers call this phenomenon *positive stress*, and it is considered to be highly essential for learning. "Finally, psychology and neuroscience both indicate that linking learning with students' interests is not a luxury, but a necessity" (Tomlinson & Sousa, 2020, p. 20).

NEURO-LINK: Emotions may be connected to the learning segment for life (Heath & Heath, 2018; Varlas, 2018).

Emerging evidence also suggests that whenever strong feelings are present during a learning experience, those emotions may be connected to the learning in the student's brain forever. Quoting Immordino-Yang, Varlas highlights this point: "It's literally neurobiologically impossible to remember or think deeply about anything that you haven't felt emotion about" (Varlas, 2018, para. 4). Heath and Heath (2018) support this notion as well through their discussion about peak moments and claim that schooling today is largely absent of these emotional highs. "In order to motivate students, emotions need to be involved, and a peak moment is a great way to integrate deep emotions, preparation, the right amount of pressure, and academics" (p. 10).

To prove the strength of this principle to teachers-in-training, I have often asked them to raise their hand if they currently have either a positive or negative emotion attached to some random past learning. I, then, call out examples (e.g., learning geometry, learning a foreign language, learning to type). As soon as I mention each one of these examples, students' hands immediately are raised to signal that they do have a strong emotional feeling, either positive or negative, connected with that learning experience. This activity demonstrates that we carry these emotional "backpacks" into the future. Therefore, it remains strategic for teachers to encode the most positive emotional experiences into each learning experience as possible.

 NEURO-LINK: Brain plasticity is key to the concept of growth mindset, the understanding that intelligence can be developed and is a significant motivator for student learning (Boaler, 2013; National Academies of Sciences, Engineering, and Medicine, 2018; Sarrasin et al., 2018).

From Chapter 1 we know that the brain is constantly changing. The creation, strengthening, and pruning of neural connections are key to the learning process (National Academies of Sciences, Engineering, and Medicine, 2018). This phenomenon, known as brain plasticity, is foundational to the understanding that intelligence can be developed. Boaler (2013) contends that neuroscience has provided irrefutable evidence that the brain continuously grows and changes and that this evidence has major implications for the theory of growth mindset and why it should be taught in school to all students. This same conclusion was reached by a team of neuroscientists in a recent meta-analysis

(Sarrasin et al., 2018). "Results show that inducing a growth mindset by teaching neuroplasticity has an overall positive effect on motivation, achievement, and brain activity" (p. 31).

 NEURO-LINK: Fostering growth mindsets in students has been proven to increase student motivation, ownership of learning, and academic achievement (Kim & Park, 2021; Paunesku et al., 2015; Rattan et al., 2015; Schmidt et al., 2016; Yeager & Dweck, 2020).

Carol Dweck, a noted American psychologist and professor of psychology at Stanford University, has contributed enormously to contemporary educational practice by championing the brain's potential for growth. She is a pioneer of "the power of yet" and in spreading the word that abilities can be developed. According to Dweck (2014), a growth mindset is where learners believe that making an effort can continue improving and building their skills even if they may initially experience challenges with the subject matter. Built upon the brain's ability to continue to grow connections (brain plasticity), a growth mindset seeks to help teachers and students create a belief system that they can learn with two simple words, *not yet*, or as she calls it, *a yet mentality* (Dweck, 2014). Furthermore, Whitman and Kelleher (2016) make this astounding claim: "Mindset is often classified as one of the most critical 'noncognitive' skills that students must cultivate to meet their potential as learners and as individuals" (p. 42). Moreover, they add this important clarification: "Having a growth mindset also requires the development of clearly defined strategies for improvement and the enlistment of support, advice, and guidance from others" (p. 43).

 NEURO-LINK: Researchers have found a relationship between intrinsic motivation, which can be enhanced by having a growth mindset, and the release of dopamine in the brain (Ng, 2018).

There is more to having a growth mindset than meets the eye. Neuroscientific evidence supports the idea that individuals with a growth mindset exhibit not only resilience in facing challenges but also increased brain plasticity. Furthermore, the correlation between intrinsic motivation and the activation of reward pathways in the brain leads to increased attention, engagement, and persistence.

I would like to close this section with a quote from one of my graduate students, *"Our current education system may not be perfect, but I am hopeful that it is just not perfect YET."*

USING THIS SUPERPOWER IN YOUR CLASSROOM

Creating a safe classroom experience can be a teacher's superpower as it is so fundamentally connected to students' emotional well-being as we have learned from research studies in educational neuroscience cited earlier in this chapter. Let us now examine several ways teachers may intentionally work to create emotional safety for their students.

Classroom Meetings

Classroom meetings are a growing trend in schools today. Alternately called *classroom meetings* and *morning meetings*, this classroom structure has students' social and emotional growth as its main goal. Class meetings allow teachers and students to come together as a group to build community, solve problems, and create positive classrooms (Vance, 2013). One comment attesting to the power of morning meetings to create emotionally safe classrooms was asserted by Maurice Sykes, former deputy superintendent for the District of Columbia school system. "Morning Meeting is a silent bulldozer in the field of school reform" (Sykes, cited in Kriete, 2011, para. 14).

Meetings can be either structured or nonstructured. *Structured* classroom meetings usually have students sit in a circle to create a more inclusive configuration. The facilitator, usually the teacher, moves the group through four separate phases: (1) *greeting*, where each child greets another class-mate, generally one that is sitting next to them; (2) *sharing* something personal (e.g., how they are feeling, something they did); (3) *group activity* to build community (e.g., "I Spy" in which the teacher calls out clues to something in the room and students try to guess [thus building attention and language skills], teacher asks students to name something that begins with a specific letter, teacher asks students to share things that come in pairs, etc.); and (4) *topic of the day*, which can be either academic or directed toward social-emotional development (e.g., ways to make everyone feel welcome in our class, name an animal that lives near the water, etc.) (Kriete & Davis, 2014). *Unstructured classroom meetings* can be held at any time. Many teachers choose the end of the week for a meeting, such as a wrap-up of what has been learned.

According to Hansen (2019), classroom meetings can also have many academic and emotional benefits for secondary students as they are even more socially aware than their elementary counterparts. Some question prompts for secondary teachers are provided here.

Icebreakers

- If you had one superpower, what would it be?
- Who are your top three people you respect and why?
- If you could go anywhere in the world, where would you go?

Prompts Related to School/Class

- What could our school due to improve your educational or social experience?
- What is something you think teens understand, but adults do not?
- Can kindness be cool? Why or why not?
- How can our classroom feel more inclusive to each student?
- Name one thing that you would like to change (a) at our school and (b) in our classroom.

Classroom Meetings: One-Stop Shop

I decided to include the following resource here, as opposed to the resources section, as it has everything that teachers need to implement classroom meetings.

https://bit.ly/3MJdbDw

Growth Mindset Dos and Don'ts

Fostering students' growth mindset is something that takes patience. Teaching students how to say "not yet" is one step in that direction. Along with having high expectations for all students, growth mindset can be a true superpower. Let's examine some Dos and Don'ts.

Dos

- Hold classroom meetings to create safe spaces for students to be seen as individuals with skills and abilities.
- Create a risk-taking classroom culture with mistakes being normalized.
- Strengthen perseverance by scaffolding ways for students to approach difficult tasks.
- Instead of always correcting student errors, sometimes highlight them and allow students reflection time (perhaps with a partner) to correct the error.

Don'ts

- Just telling students to try harder without scaffolding different strategies will not produce good results. Try this suggestion from Diamond (2014) instead: "By providing scaffolds to help children exercise executive functions, children get practice, which helps their executive functions improve, and children have the pride of having succeeded (of being a good listener, for example) and increased confidence" (p. 12).

Direct Teaching and Practice of Executive Functioning Skills

Many students become anxious, not because they can't learn but because they lack organizational know-how. These skills, grouped around reflection and metacognition, are powerful tools that promote deep learning and self-awareness. When students engage in reflection, they actively think about their learning processes, evaluate their progress, and identify areas for growth. Metacognition involves being aware of one's own thinking and learning strategies. By incorporating reflective practices, such as journaling, self-assessment, and goal-setting, educators can encourage students to take ownership of their learning journey. Through reflection, students understand concepts, make connections, and transfer knowledge to real-world situations. Additionally, metacognition enhances problem-solving skills and equips students with strategies to regulate their learning. By fostering a culture of reflection and metacognition, educators empower students to become self-directed learners who can continually improve their learning outcomes.

- Teach metacognitive executive function skills-planning, working memory/updating, problem-solving, self-monitoring, mental flexibility, generativity/fluency, and inhibition.

  » Ask students *"How do you study for a test?"* and then break them into small groups to share their answers.

  » Teach study techniques to students, emphasizing recall and not just rereading notes.

  » Teach note-taking skills.

    - Have pairs of students practice with a paragraph trying to identify the key points.

    - Provide a fill-in template for students to take notes, and give a lecture so students may practice.

    - Invite students to create a day-by-day plan for a longer project.

- Create a problem-solving anchor chart with students, and practice using it in class with mock problems.
- Have students identify their personal "hard spots" in completing school work or homework.

SUPERPOWERED RESOURCES

 Websites

• Mindset Works

https://www.mindsetworks.com/free-resources/

Mindset Works is the global leader in growth mindset development, leveraging the pioneering research of Carol Dweck and Lisa Blackwell. The company's mission is to enable a world where everyone realizes continual learning and growth.

• Family Newsletter for Mindset

https://bit.ly/3FVyQF0

Videos

• Carol Dweck: Teaching a Growth Mindset

https://www.youtube.com/watch?v=isHM1rEd3GE

In this talk, Carol Dweck describes two ways to think about a problem that's slightly too hard for you to solve. Are you not smart enough to solve it? Or have you just not solved it yet?

• The Power of Relationships in School

https://bit.ly/47ab1Ff

- How Puppets Can Help Kids Express Emotions

https://bit.ly/3FYZgWl

 Books/Articles

- 11 Picture Books to Help Young Students Manage Their Worries

https://bit.ly/46dsCLe

- 5 Research-Backed Studying Techniques

https://bit.ly/3sxyfpQ

- How to Counter Learned Helplessness

https://bit.ly/3QGRw0h

- 3 Collaborative Strategies to Build Up Students' Note-Taking Skills

https://bit.ly/47yS9j0

- A De-escalation Exercise for Upset Students

https://bit.ly/3ulu1lC

- How Teachers Can Empower Students Who Are Experiencing Trauma

https://bit.ly/3QYdkoj

- Dweck, C. (2008). *Mindsets and math/science achievement*. Carnegie Corporation of New York, Institute for Advanced Study, Commission on Mathematics and Science Education.

- Immordino-Yang, M. H., Darling-Hammond, L., & Krone, C. R. (2019). Nurturing nature: How brain development is inherently social and emotional, and what this means for education. *Educational Psychologist*, *54*(3), 185–204. https://doi.org/10.1080/00461520.2019.1633924

- Li, L., Isherwood Gow, A. D., & Zhou, J. (2020). The role of positive emotions in education: A neuroscience perspective. *Mind, Brain, and Education*, *14*(3), 220–233.

REFERENCES

Boaler, J. (2013). Ability and mathematics: The mindset revolution that is reshaping education. *Forum: For Promoting 3-19 Comprehensive Education*, *55*(1), 143–152.

Desautels, L. (2023). *The power of reframing to "rewire" students' brains*. Edutopia. https://www.edutopia.org/article/reframing-rewire-student-brains

Diamond, A. (2014). Want to optimize executive functions and academic outcomes? Simple, just nourish the human spirit. *Minnesota Symposia on Child Psychology*, *37*, 205–232.

Dweck, C. (2014). *The power of believing that you can improve* [Video]. TED Conferences. https://www.ted.com/talks/carol_dweck_the_power_of_believing_that_you_can_improve?language=en

Hansen, C. B. (2019). *The heart and science of teaching: Transformative applications that integrate academic and social–emotional learning*. Teachers College Press.

Heath, C., & Heath, D. (2018, January 10). The secret to student engagement. *Education Week*. https://www.edweek.org/leadership/opinion-the-secret-to-student-engagement/2018/01?cmp=eml-eb-wel1.12&M=58405914&U=2735312

Immordino-Yang, M. H., & Damasio, A. (2007). We feel, therefore we learn: The relevance of affective and social neuroscience to education. *Mind, Brain, and Education*, *1*(1), 3–10.

Immordino-Yang, M. H., Darling-Hammond, L., & Krone, C. R. (2018). *The Brain Basis for Integrated Social, Emotional, and Academic Development: How Emotions and Social Relationships Drive Learning*. Aspen Institute.

Kim, M. S., & Park, S. (2021). Growth of fixed mindset from elementary to middle school: Its relationship with trajectories of academic behavior engagement and academic achievement. *Psychology in the Schools*, *58*(11), 2175–2188. https://doi.org/10.1002/pits.22583

Kriete, R. (2011, July 20). *The power of morning meeting*. Responsive Classroom. https://www.responsiveclassroom.org/the-power-of-morning-meeting

Kriete, R., & Davis, C. (2014). *The morning meeting book* (3rd ed.). Center for Responsive Schools.

National Academies of Sciences, Engineering, and Medicine. (2018). *How people learn II: Learners, contexts, and cultures*. https://nap.nationalacademies.org/catalog/24783/how-people-learn-ii-learners-contexts-and-cultures

Ng, B. (2018). The neuroscience of growth mindset and intrinsic motivation. *Brain Sciences*, *8*(2), 20–30. https://doi.org/10.3390/brainsci8020020

Paunesku, D., Walton, G. M., Romero, C., Smith, E. N., Yeager, D. S., & Dweck, C. S. (2015). Mindset interventions are a scalable treatment for academic underachievement. *Psychological Science*, *26*(6), 784–793. https://doi.org/10.1177/0956797615571017

Rattan, A., Savani, K., Chugh, D., & Dweck, C. S. (2015). Leveraging mindsets to promote academic achievement. *Perspectives on Psychological Science*, *10*(6), 721–726. https://doi.org/10.1177/1745691615599383

Sarrasin, J. B., Nenciovici, L., Foisy, L. M. B., Allaire-Duquette, G., Riopel, M., Masson, S. (2018). Effects of teaching the concept of neuroplasticity to induce a growth mindset on motivation, achievement, and brain activity: A meta-analysis. *Trends in Neuroscience and Education*, *12*, 22–31. https://doi.org/10.1016/j.tine.2018.07.003

Schmidt, J. A., Shumow, L., & Kackar-Cam, H. Z. (2016). Does mindset intervention predict students' daily experience in classrooms? A comparison of seventh and ninth graders' trajectories. *Journal of Youth and Adolescence*, *46*(3), 582–602. https://doi.org/10.1007/s10964-016-0489-z

Sousa, D., & Tomlinson, C. (2018). *Differentiation and the brain: How neuroscience supports the learner-friendly classroom* (2nd ed.). ASCD.

Tomlinson, C., & Sousa, D. (2020, May). The sciences of learning. *Educational Leadership*. *77*(8), 14–20.

Tyng, C. M., Amin, H. U., Saad, M. N. M., & Malik, A. S. (2017). The influences of emotion on learning and memory. *Frontiers in Psychology*, *8*, 1454.

Vance, E. (2013). Preschool through grade 1: Class meeting variations and adaptations. *Young Children*, *5*(42), 42–45.

Varlas, L. (2018). Emotions are the rudder that steers thinking. *ASCD: Education Update*, *60*(6). https://www.ascd.org/el/articles/emotions-are-the-rudder-that-steers-thinking

Whitman, G., & Kelleher, I. (2016). *Neuroteach: Brain science and the future of education*. Rowman & Littlefield.

Willis, J. (2021, February). The neuroscience of joyful learning. *ISA Journal*, (24). https://issuu.com/bainespsa/docs/a76891_isa_journal_issue_24_issuu/s/11678932

Yeager, D. S., & Dweck, C. S. (2020). What can be learned from growth mindset controversies? *American Psychologist*, *75*(9), 1269–1284. https://doi.org/10.1037/amp0000794

NOTES

COLLABORATION:
THE BRAIN-TO-BRAIN LEARNING BOOST

Cooperative learning is a brain turn-on.

–Willis (2007)

In Chapter 3, we examined how your understanding of the connection between emotion and cognition can be a superpower. Let us explore the social dimension of learning, that is, the other half of the social-emotional learning (SEL) dynamic duo. Learning can, of course, be undertaken individually. However, learning *in school* is, by nature, a social endeavor! Cooperative/collaborative learning has been among the most investigated instructional practices ever. Kagan (2014) asserts, "Over 1,000 studies demonstrate the positive effects of cooperative learning on academic achievement, social/emotional development, cognitive development, liking for school and class, as well as a host of other positive outcomes" (para. 9).

WHAT MAKES COLLABORATION A SUPERPOWER? EXAMINING THE RESEARCH

Neuroscientists can now shed light on why student-to-student collaboration can provide an extra boost to the teaching–learning equation.

 NEURO-LINK: The human brain is wired for social interactions (Clark & Dumas, 2015; Jazuli et al., 2019; Willis, 2015).

Early 20th-century psychologists (Dewey, 1938; Piaget, 1932; Vygotsky, 1978) believed there was an essential social aspect to learning and the brain's development. DeVries (1997) wrote, "For Piaget, therefore, cooperation is an essential characteristic of developmentally oriented education not simply because it is a culturally valued virtue, but because of its psychodynamic, developmental significance" (p. 6).

What is it about social interactions in school that elevates their significance to this degree and, with appropriate use by teachers, may even be called a *superpower?* The answer to the question is twofold. First, there is a learning boost that is provided by positive and supportive relationships. This finding relates to Caine and Caine's Principle #1 for how the brain works (mentioned in Chapter 1), *The brain/mind is social.* Second, content-related discussions with one or more students add an auditory input to the brain, thus creating additional dendritic connections for long-term memory retrieval.

 NEURO-LINK: Positive peer-to-peer interactions during collaborative learning stimulate the learning networks and help control the brain's fear-based response in the amygdala of fight, flight, or freeze (Johnson & Johnson, 2006; Marzano et al., 2001; Willis, 2022).

We are reminded by Willis (2022) of the brain boost that occurs for students during collaborative work in the classroom: "The interactive and interdependent components of cooperative learning offer the emotional and interpersonal experiences needed to stimulate the development of the prefrontal cortex networks that direct successful communication, collaboration, adaptation, and resilience" (para. 2). However, the benefits to students' growth in critical social-emotional skills have been investigated for the past three decades, and the results have stayed consistently high. In fact, in the meta-analyses of hundreds of research studies on cooperative learning, Marzano et al. (2001) affirmed that not only was cooperative learning a highly effective instructional routine for student achievement but it also provided students with a way of feeling socially and emotionally supported by their peers.

USING THIS SUPERPOWER IN YOUR CLASSROOM

As early as the 1980s, researchers began to promote social strategies that were then categorized by the label *cooperative learning*. Today we have added the term *collaborative learning*. Some researchers have made efforts to define each of these terms. However, many educators feel that these two terms may be used interchangeably as their strength lies in students working in pairs or small groups, with some autonomy and choice, to accomplish a learning task. For this discussion, I will use the abbreviation CL to refer to both cooperative and collaborative learning.

When CL first appeared in schools, it was seen as a most unwelcome innovation by teachers and parents as it contradicted practices that had been in place for more than 100 years—notably that students should sit still, listen to the teacher, and complete their work in isolation from their peers. However, a vast body of research over 20 years confirms CL has a positive effect on learning in all content disciplines (Gillies, 2016; Hattie, 2012; Johnson & Johnson, 2009; Kagan, 2014). In the United States today, we are approaching nearly 100% of teachers who use some form of CL structures in their classrooms due mainly to the overwhelming achievement gains that it affords.

There are dozens of ways for you to construct a collaborative learning environment, from the simple *partner talk*, to the more elaborate *jigsaw* teaching models (Aronson, 1978), where students become experts with a portion of the content and, in small groups, take turns teaching one another the whole. Let us explore some of these models.

SIMPLE GROUP–LEARNING SUPERPOWERED TOOLS

- **Pair-Share** remains one of the easiest yet most effective of all cooperative learning tools. It is easy as there is no set-up other than creating an organized way for students to be paired up. It is emotionally safe for students, as only one other person will hear (and maybe) judge the response. Moreover, it is highly effective and on-task as all students (and not just the select few students who tend to answer most classroom questions) can answer *every* question. I want to stress that the simplicity of this structure does not belie the power of its effectiveness. Research from educational neuroscience demonstrates that students need to do something active for the information to move through the brain. Furthermore, talking is a form of active learning. When more students can become actively engaged in answering most classroom questions (upward of 300 a day, researchers have observed), this structure becomes an actual superpower.

- **Triads** are an off-shoot of the pair-share structure with the addition of a third member to the group. The rule of cooperative learning is that the smaller the group, the more emotional safety and higher engagement. Moreover, the larger the group size, the more opportunities for many ideas to be shared; however, some learners may become disengaged. For these reasons, triads are considered a near-perfect group size. It is small enough for students to feel safe, yet the third person offers more ideas and solutions.

- **Pair-Squared** is a grouping of four students, but it does not just involve adding a fourth member. Pair-squared is a structured conversation with its own rules. It is similar to pair-share, but two pairs share their responses to the prompt after the initial paired conversation. Both teachers and students find pair-squared to be an engaging cooperative learning strategy as it retains the safety levels of pair-share but also allows for the discussion to become deeper and more nuanced.

- **World Café** is a conversational group activity where students in groups sit at tables around the classroom ("café tables") and discuss a prompt or question provided by the teacher. When the bell rings, students move to a new table of their choice and engage with a different question. Usually, chart paper is placed on the tables to capture the discussion points for the debriefing that takes place at the end of the activity.

- **Four Corners** allows students some choice as they move to one of the four corners of the classroom to engage in a topic or opinion.

  » An elementary teacher might identify four inventions (airplanes, automobiles, television, computers) and designate one of the four corners of the classroom to match each one. Students physically move to the invention/corner they select as the most important invention and work with their peers to develop evidence for their claim and then share it with the class.

  » In a secondary biology classroom, a teacher might ask, "Choose one of the following four macromolecules: carbohydrates, lipids, proteins, or nucleic acids. Then, move to the corresponding corner of the room and, with others who have chosen this macromolecule, research the interactions in the human body."

⚡ MULTIFACETED GROUP LEARNING STRATEGIES

Project-Based Learning (PBL)

John Dewey has been credited by many as the founder of project-based learning as he promoted a learning approach based on experiences related to real life outside of school. Today, due to the amassing of many research studies demonstrating the learning potential of PBL, there is a resurgence of interest and excitement in this pedagogy, which has led to the robust accumulation of examples of projects on the internet. Here are some organizations that share ideas with teachers.

- PBL Units for Middle and High School

  » **Art: Art as Activism**

    In groups, students will research how artists communicate their activism through their work and create a classroom museum to display social justice works of art.

» **Math: Which Cell Phone Plan Is Best?**

This PBL unit intends to raise awareness regarding cell phone prices, plans, and, most importantly, digital citizenship. Students will compare family plans and suggest an appropriate plan for their family's needs. In teams, students conduct research on cell phone use that includes visiting a cell phone service provider, parent interviews, peer surveys, and analysis of various service plans. Students will first present their findings to each other in class. Students will create Google Slide presentations for an audience of parents, peers, teachers, and school staff. Students will explain and justify the best family plan based on their findings.

» **Science: Electricity Innovation**

Students reflect on the consistent presence of electricity in their life and their power consumption and explore problems that involve the application of electricity as they design and construct an innovation that enhances a user's experience and consumes minimal power.

» **Science: Periodic Table Storybook**

In groups, students create a children's storybook about an element on the periodic table and explain the location of the part (column, group, atomic number, atomic mass, protons, neutrons, electrons, periodic trends, etc.); the types of bonds the element forms, including descriptions of these bonds; common compounds that this element forms; and how the part is used in everyday life.

» **Social Science: Build a Museum**

Students create a museum. This museum will be about Egyptian history. Students will use the question formulation technique (QFT) to develop a part of Egyptian history they want to study and learn more about. Questions students might ask could relate to Egyptian sport, architecture, fashion, and animal husbandry. Students will focus on finding a topic and question that interests them.

» **Social Science/Science: World Problem**

Students will plan, design, and create a machine or tool that solves a world problem.

- PBL Units for Elementary Grades.

  » **Social Studies/ELA: Perspectives of Black Civil Rights Members**

  In this project, students access primary sources to learn about the experiences and perspectives of individuals in the Black civil rights movement.

» **Science/Math/ELA: Let's Build a Restaurant**

In groups, students will design a restaurant for low-income communities that is both healthy and affordable. The critical issue is that communities need access to restaurants that are affordable, offer healthy options, and use sustainable practices.

» **Science/ELA: Environmental Waste**

In groups, students will research and create a plan to educate the community about the impacts of waste on the environment and what can be done to reduce waste.

» **Science/Engineering: Shelters**

Students use their knowledge of two-dimensional and three-dimensional shapes to explore and recreate structures used as homes to create a shelter suitable for living.

Role-Playing

Role-playing is a teaching strategy that fits within the social family of models (Joyce et al., 2000). These strategies emphasize the social nature of learning and see cooperative behavior stimulating students socially and intellectually. Role-playing can be used in any content area and is appropriate for grade levels PK–12.

• Reenactment of a historical event

• Scene from a book or story

• Newspaper article

• Science symposium

• Classroom management situation

• Math problem

• Conversation between historical figures

• Life in early times

• Scientific discovery

Jigsaw Learning

This potent cooperative learning structure got its name from the analogy of a jigsaw puzzle, where every piece is essential to completing the puzzle task (Aronson, 1978). Likewise, the jigsaw group strategy creates a condition where every student in the group is critical to achieving the learning task. It is useful when a topic or problem is complex and involves multiple perspectives. To start, students are placed in identified jigsaw groups with diversity among abilities, cultures, and ethnicities. A group size of four to six students is ideal.

Each group member takes responsibility for mastering a small component of the learning segment. Following the formation of the jigsaw groups, expert groups are formed, composed of students who have been assigned the same part. The function of the expert group is to strengthen each student's knowledge of the topic and, thus, their confidence in presenting the information to their jigsaw group. Once the expert groups have completed learning the material, they are disbanded. Students rejoin their original jigsaw team and take turns teaching their part to the other members (Aronson, 1978).

SUPERPOWERED RESOURCES

Additional resources (websites, videos, and books/articles) to encourage cooperative/collaborative are provided for you in this section.

💻 Websites

Many U.S. universities sponsor cooperative learning/group work websites that articulate research and practical ideas for utilizing these practices in the K–16 classroom. Following is a listing of five of the most notable ones.

- Center for Research on Learning and Teaching

https://bit.ly/4691gpG

- The Center for Innovation in Teaching & Learning (CITL)

https://bit.ly/3MDS19R

- Derek Bok Center for Teaching and Learning

https://bit.ly/3FZ8d1R

- Harvard University, ABLConnect

https://bit.ly/3FZ8hi7

Videos

The following videos have been chosen to provide classroom examples of SEL and collaborative learning practices.

- Cooperative Learning: Strategies for Educators

https://bit.ly/3svvjdr

- Getting All Students to Participate

https://bit.ly/3SH1GjY

- Learning on Their Feet

https://bit.ly/3QCvtYu

- The Social Classroom

https://bit.ly/3QLMDTI

- How to Play Crumple and Shoot

https://bit.ly/3MKquUy

- Collaborative Learning Builds Deeper Understanding

https://bit.ly/3ud2pzc

- 60-Second Strategy: Cooperative Learning Roles

https://bit.ly/3SGNzvc

- Encouraging Academic Conversation With Talk Moves

https://bit.ly/49AUb44

- How to Use the Reciprocal Learning Strategy

https://bit.ly/3ud31F0

- City Plan: Project-Based Learning

https://bit.ly/47bkRXG

Books/Articles

- How to: The Jigsaw Method Revisited

https://bit.ly/3R1UOg0

- Four Strategies to Improve Group Work

https://bit.ly/47cTvjQ

- Deeper Learning: Collaboration Is Key

https://bit.ly/3ulIcHm

- A Starting Point for Kagan Cooperative Learning

https://bit.ly/3uhnngr

- A Strategy for Boosting Student Engagement in Math

https://bit.ly/46htLS5

- A World of Project Ideas (You Can Steal)

https://bit.ly/47v6RHZ

A compendium of PBL ideas and driving questions for TK–12 teachers

- What the Heck Is Project-Based Learning?

https://bit.ly/49AWrs4

- The Role of PBL in Making the Shift to Common Core

https://bit.ly/3QXHN6Z

- What Is PBL?

http://bie.org/about/what_pbl

- How Are Projects and Project-Based Learning Different?

https://bit.ly/40ADsK9

- Debunking Five Myths About Project-Based Learning

- How to Write Effective Driving Questions for Project-Based Learning

https://bit.ly/40DfnlQ

https://bit.ly/3MJu54W

REFERENCES

Aronson, E. (Ed.). (1978). *The jigsaw classroom*. SAGE.

Clark, I., & Dumas, G. (2015). Toward a neural basis for peer-interaction: What makes peer-learning tick? *Frontiers in Psychology*, *6*, Article 28. https://doi.org/10.3389/fpsyg.2015.00028

DeVries, R. (1997). Piaget's social theory. *Educational Researcher*, *26*(2), 4–17. https://doi.org/10.3102/0013189X026002004.

Dewey, J. (1938). *Experience and education*. Macmillan.

Gillies, R. M. (2016). Cooperative learning: Review of research and practice. *Australian Journal of Teacher Education*, *41*(3), Article 3. https://ro.ecu.edu.au/cgi/viewcontent.cgi?article=2902&context=ajte

Hattie, J. (2012). *Visible learning for teachers: Maximizing impact on learning.* Routledge.

Jazuli, L. O. A., Solihatin, E., & Syahrial, Z. (2019). The effects of brain-based learning and project-based learning strategies on student group mathematics learning outcomes student visual learning styles. *Pedagogical Research*, *4*(4), em0047.

Johnson, D. W., & Johnson, F. P. (2006). *Joining together: Group theory and group skills* (9th ed.). Allyn & Bacon.

Johnson, D. W., & Johnson, R. T. (2009). An educational psychology success story: Social interdependence theory and cooperative learning. *Educational Researcher*, *38*(5), 365–379. https://doi.org/10.3102/0013189X09339057

Joyce, B. R., Weil, M., & Calhoun, E. (2000). *Models of teaching* (6th ed.). Allyn & Bacon.

Kagan, S. (2014, Winter). *Effect size reveals the impact of Kagan structures and cooperative learning*. https://www.kaganonline.com/free_articles/dr_spencer_kagan/384/Effect-Size-Reveals-the-Impact-of-Kagan-Structures-and-Cooperative-Learning

Marzano, R. J., Pickering, D. J., & Pollock, J. E. (2001). *Classroom instruction that works: Research-based strategies for increasing student achievement*. Association for Supervision and Curriculum Development.

Piaget, J. (1932). *The moral judgment of the child*. Free Press.

Vygotsky, L. S. (1978). *Mind in society: The development of higher psychological processes*. Harvard University Press.

Willis, J. (2007). Cooperative learning is a brain turn-on. *Middle School Journal*, *38*(4), 4–13.

Willis, J. (2015, January). *The high cost of neuromyths in education*. Edutopia. https://www.edutopia.org/blog/high-costs-neuromyths-in-education-judy-willis

Willis, J. (2022). The neuro-science behind how cooperative learning augments social-emotional learning skills. *ed Magazine*, (20). https://newsletter.globalcitizenshipfoundation.org/p/issue-20-transforming-education-newsletter-953014

NOTES

MAKING IT STICKY:
BOOSTING LONG-TERM MEMORY

When my students forget from day-to-day (short-term memory) and from year-to-year (long-term memory) can I just blame their distracted brains? Or is there a teaching issue here?

–Sprenger (2018)

I have become keenly aware of how trivial some perceive a pleasurable learning experience to be. However, this is the key to what will make learning stick for a student.

–Teacher (2023)

Learning is a continuous process that is simultaneously cultural and biological. One common goal for all teachers is seeing their students' learning *stick*. This goal means that every teacher wishes to see that every student has grasped what they are being taught and can remember it in their time of need. Therefore, making learning "sticky" must be a top priority for teachers across all grade levels and content disciplines. Chapter 5 will focus on the neurobiological factors of long-term memory storage. As Tokuhama-Espinosa (2017) states, "Most school learning requires well-functioning working, short- and long-term memory systems and conscious attention" (p. 45). Specific, high-yield instructional practices will be featured that are most likely to increase student learning.

WHAT MAKES STICKY LEARNING A SUPERPOWER: EXAMINING THE RESEARCH

Since the beginning of schooling, teachers have struggled to help students remember what they have just been taught. According to classic studies on forgetting, 50% of new memory fades in the brain after 20 minutes and 70% after 24 hours (Ebbinghaus, 1964). Since the mid-1960s, researchers have sought to identify factors that would make a difference in the seemingly inevitable forgetting that happens for all learners.

Our brains are adept at receiving, filtering, consolidating, and storing learning for both the short and long term. The hippocampus is the brain's memory center where this activity is centered. Whitman and Kelleher (2016) share the neuroscience behind these processes: "In the hippocampus, neurons are created and undergo strengthening, pruning, and remodeling during learning" (p. 36). To say this another way, when students are learning, the neurons in their brains create pathways. Furthermore, when students continue to use these pathways repeatedly, they are strengthened, thus creating linkages for long-term memories to form. When pathways are first formed but not continually used, they are pruned away as they are identified by the brain as no longer being needed. That is where the saying "use it or lose it" comes into play.

Heath and Heath (2018) suggest that if the brain encounters new information in a passive state, it will result in passive learning (where there is a slight chance that it will make it to your long-term memory). However, if students become active learners through movement and multisensory experiences, they will experience a greater chance of remembering.

Sprenger (2018) shared seven phases in the lesson sequence to significantly reduce predictable forgetting. She termed these the "7 Rs" (Figure 5.1).

- *Reach.* The first requirement is to help students "reach" into their brains to focus on incoming sensory information.

- *Reflect.* Once we have found a way for students to "pay attention," we need to cue them to spend a moment or two in reflection, which activates cognition.

- *Recode.* After reflection comes a most potent component: putting the information into their own words. I know of a school district that found great success in their high schools with what they termed the "*10–2*" strategy. Teachers were encouraged to lecture for only 10 minutes at a time, then find a way for students to put the information in their own words, either orally with a partner or written into a journal or notebook.

- *Reinforce.* During this formative assessment step, teachers check in with students to ensure they have accurately recoded the information.

Figure 5.1 Sprenger 7Rs (2018)

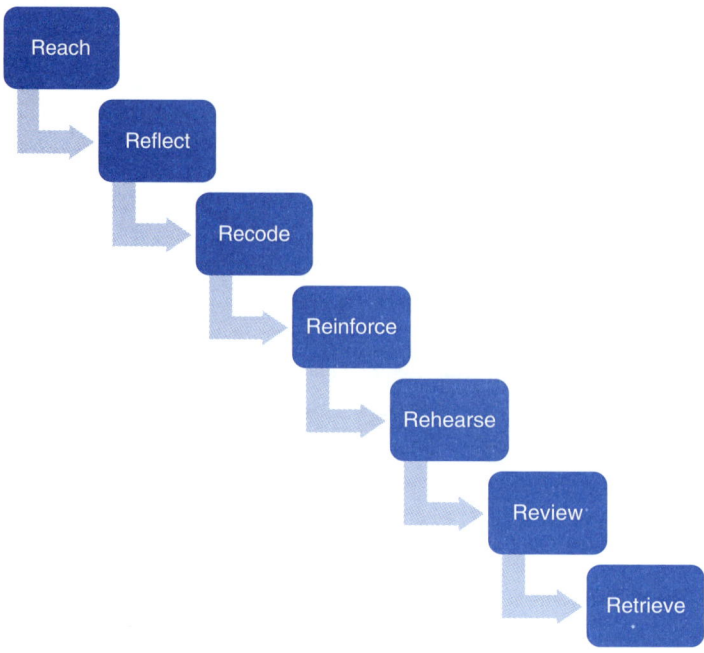

- *Rehearse & Review.* I am placing Sprenger's fifth and sixth steps together because they are closely aligned and essential. We all know how easy it is to forget someone's name at a social function. However, if we take a few moments to say their name repeatedly (rehearsal) or, better yet, review it later, we are more likely to remember it. Repetition also causes a substance called myelin to grow around newly formed neural pathways, helping them fire together to automate a new skill or mental connection (Bengtsson et al., 2005).

- *Retrieve.* As we will note in Chapter 8 on assessing student learning, having students actively retrieve stored information reminds the brain to keep this particular data point in a place where it is easily found. In addition, quizzing ourselves on new learning (*self-evaluation*) and straining to recall new learning (*retrieval practice*) supports long-term memory better than typical (but largely ineffective) strategies like rereading, highlighting text, or writing summaries (Dunlosky et al., 2013).

Looking holistically at the 7 Rs, Sprenger claims that most teachers overlook the two steps *reflect* and *recode*, primarily due to lack of time. However, when one thinks about the time lost to reteaching forgotten information, employing the power of reflection and recoding may be worth the effort to support students' long-term memory formation.

NEURO-LINK: Teaching to a student's "supposed" learning style is not supported by neuroscience. However, providing students with a variety of modalities (auditory, visual, kinesthetic, tactile) with which to encode and practice new learnings is a predictor of more robust memory storage (Tullis, 2023; Whitman & Kelleher, 2016).

One of the more persistent instructional myths is related to learning styles. Neuroscience now confirms that, while individuals do have some learning preferences, long-term memory is enhanced when information is presented, practiced, and demonstrated in a variety of learning modalities, such as auditory, visual, kinesthetic, and movement (Whitman & Kelleher, 2016). Tullis (2023) confirms this fact in a more cognitively detailed explanation: "Processing information in multiple and varied forms (including multiple senses, abstract and concrete representations, diverse examples, and varied activities) creates elaborated and detailed memories, which enhances the long-term retention and generalization of that knowledge" (para. 6).

 NEURO-LINK: Memory is affected by emotional connections (Mammarella et al., 2014; Tomlinson & Sousa, 2020; Tyng et al., 2017).

One of the most exciting neuroscience contributions to classroom instruction derives from new understandings about emotions' role in learning. New learning without an emotional charge will not likely be stored long term (Tyng et al., 2017). Tomlinson and Sousa (2020) add their interpretation of the critical role of emotions: "Emotions are a gateway to cognition and learning. When curriculum and instruction evoke enjoyment, surprise, empathy, personal relevance, and so forth, the gateway opens, and learning is likely to proceed more effectively and durably" (para. 19). What an astounding revelation! Teachers no longer have to feel guilty going "off plan" when students laugh, play a game, or enjoy a peak moment of insight regarding the content topic at hand.

Similarly, teaching content through stories, as in using biographies to teach history, can evoke emotional connections as different areas of the brain are activated than when we learn facts. When we listen to a story, dopamine and oxytocin are released. These two chemicals affect motivation and attention and allow the listener to stay attentive to the story, making it more meaningful. As Hasson (2016) explains, "A story is the only way to activate parts of the brain so that a listener turns the story into their own idea and experience" (transcript para. 16).

NEURO-LINK: Providing opportunities for students to recall newly acquired material, learning has a more substantial chance of becoming long term (Agarwal et al., 2021; Dunlosky et al., 2013).

Classroom teachers have a variety of ways to slow down forgetting and assist students in encoding the information for a more extended period. Some of these techniques are spacing, interleaving, and testing.

- *Spacing:* We learn concepts and recall information better if we study them in multiple spread-out sessions. We can acquire any knowledge and achieve mastery if we practice spaced repetition. Spaced learning sessions do not have to be tedious; all a person needs is 30 minutes daily. Ebbinghaus also emphasized the intensity of emotions and attention regarding memory retention. While Mammarella and colleagues' (2014) study confirmed that positive and negative emotions generated strong spacing effects in learning, Vlach et al. (2008) found that attention was not the primary cause of the spacing effect.

- *Interleaving:* Interleaving is setting up classroom opportunities for students to switch back and forth between recalling information just learned and previously learned. Many studies have confirmed that this method is beneficial in forming long-term memories. Math is one subject where textbook publishers intentionally include previously learned information in assessments for new content.

- *Testing:* Testing is mentioned earlier as one of the three ways to promote memory retention. Testing as a "retrieval practice" supports learners in recalling information by creating dendritic pathways leading to the information. Teachers need to consider student needs and classroom context when generating testing questions. Also, for testing to be an effective form of memory retrieval, the more they are low-stakes (self-checking) instead of high-stakes (for grades), the better they will work (Immordino-Yang et al., 2019).

 NEURO-LINK: Arts-based instructional strategies aid long-term retention of information (Rinne et al., 2011).

Research studies from as far back as 1932 through present times have underscored the power of the arts to aid in the retention of information. These studies demonstrate how the arts work in concert (pun intended) with what we now know to be the optimum conditions for long-term memories to form and include the capability of learners to engage in one or more of the following:

- *Repeated rehearsal:* Everyone knows that rehearsing is a big part of dramatic performances. Integrating standards-based content into a play boosts memory because students participate in several rehearsals (Craik & Watkins, 1973).

- *Elaboration:* Retention is enhanced when learners add details to their learning. Connecting newly learned content to art (e.g., a drawing, a play, a song) allows the brain to create more dendritic connections (Rinne et al., 2011).

- *Creation of new information:* Retention is enhanced when learners add original information to that presented via textbook or teacher. This principle underpins the positive effects of closure during a lesson where students either compose an exit ticket or discuss with a partner some takeaway from the learning episode (Rinne et al., 2011).

- *Arousal of emotions:* As was established in Chapter 2, when new learning is paired with a strong emotional response, long-term retention is more likely. The arts are unique in their capacity to arouse emotions. Therefore, teachers who intentionally incorporate arts-based expressions (visual, musical, dramatic, movement, or digital) into their lessons increase the possibility of long-term retention (Rinne et al., 2011).

USING THIS SUPERPOWER IN YOUR CLASSROOM

There are many ways that teachers can hinder the dreaded forgetting curve and influence students' long-term memory formation. Following are some examples.

The Power of Using Comparison and Contrast

Comparison is one of *the* most effective teaching strategies for student retention (Marzano et al., 2001). It is also an uncomplicated strategy as learners can compare almost anything (e.g., numbers, letters, words, shapes, trees, animals, planets, books, characters, elements, nations, art forms, movements, etc.) Some ways to have students engage in comparative thinking include the following:

- Verbal response: "What might be one way that Florida and California are alike?"

- Written response: "On your exit ticket, please write one similarity and one difference between the following two characters in our book (story or book title)."

- Classification with objects: "Put these shapes (or mineral samples, or mixtures, or leaves) into different groups that have something in common with one another."
- Venn diagram: "With your partner, create a Venn diagram showing the similarities and differences between whales and dolphins."
- Analogy: "Think of three ways the brain is like a tree."

The Power of Summarizing

Summarization is also a high-yield instructional strategy (Hattie, 2008). Long-term memory is greatly facilitated when students are tasked with creating a summary of their learning *in their own words*. Many teachers have seen the learning bump that exit tickets provide and have now integrated this routine into their daily classroom practice. *Exit tickets* require students to briefly summarize a learning segment, thus reactivating and strengthening dendrites that may have just begun to be formed. Summarization can take many forms. Examples include the following:

- Written: Students take a moment at the end of a lesson to jot down a sentence that captures what they learned or briefly respond in writing to a teacher's prompt. These exit slips may be submitted to the teacher or written in students' journals.
- Oral: Students may turn to a partner to share a lesson summary or participate in a *whip-around* that invites all students to briefly summarize their learning.
- Drawing: Students may create a sketch that relates to their learning.
- Digital: The teacher may use a digital app and have students (anonymously) add a summary comment to display for all to see.

The Power of Visuals

Everyone has heard the saying, "A picture is worth a thousand words." The truth of this wisdom lies in the power of the brain's visual processing centers. Researchers at the University of Rochester uncovered evidence that about 50% of the surface of our brain, the cortex, processes visual stimuli (Hagan, 2012). It is no wonder that visuals support memory formation and retention in learners. Even if teachers do not immediately connect to neuroscience, many have embraced visual instructional strategies because they see evidence of student learning. Examples of these structures include:

- Graphic organizers: According to the Learning Disabilities Association of America (n.d.), graphic organizers are "visual thinking tools that make pictures of your thoughts. The pictures demonstrate relationships between facts, concepts, or ideas and guide your thinking as you design the map or diagram" (para. 1). There are hundreds of different graphic organizers, but the most common are mind maps, Venn diagrams, matrices, and flow charts.

- Pictures: With the virtually unlimited resources of the internet, it is possible to *show and tell* just about any example of a lesson's content through a photo or drawing.

The Power of Arts-Based Techniques

Included in the visual and performing arts (VAPA) are four domains:

1. Visual Arts

2. Dance/Movement

3. Drama

4. Music

Each of these domains may support academic long-term memory in the four major content disciplines (math, science, social studies, and language arts). Table 5.1 showcases these connections.

Table 5.1   Teaching Content Through the Arts

Discipline	Visual Arts	Dance/ Movement	Music	Drama
Science	*Insects* Have students make insects out of clay and label body parts. *Animal Migrations* Have students use stamping kits to show tracks when learning animal migration patterns. *Periodic Table* In groups, have	*States of Matter* Have students create movements relative to the three states of matter (solid, liquid, gas). *Simple Machines* Have students move their bodies to simulate simple	*Various Topics* Have students write and perform songs about different units of science (i.e., planets, water cycle, geology, skeletal system). *Sound* Have students make different instruments out of everyday materials (e.g.,	*Water Cycle* Have students dramatize the water cycle. *Animals* Have students play charades. (What animal am I?) *Newton's Laws of Motion* Have

(Continued)

Table 5.1 Teaching Content Through the Arts (Continued)

Discipline	Visual Arts	Dance/ Movement	Music	Drama
	students create visual representations for each element of the periodic table. ***Landforms*** Have students locate classic paintings that depict landforms.	machines (inclined plane, lever, wedge, wheel and axle, pulley, and screw).	boxes, rubber bands, straws, soda cans).	students act out Newton's three laws of motion.
Social Studies	Have students paint pictures of themselves and their family members at the beginning of the school year. Have students work in groups to analyze classical paintings that depict important events in American history (e.g., *Washington Crossing the Delaware*, by Emanuel Leutze). Have students create a mosaic using the lyrics of the "Star-Spangled Banner" to dive deep into the significance and	All cultures embody movement and rhythm. Teach traditional dances representative of different cultures. Have students move to cardinal directions on a map (e.g., take three steps to the North then, skip two times to the West).	Use music as a theme and have students locate music from different periods in U.S. history. Incorporate musicals into content (e.g., *Hamilton*). Have students compose songs that tell the story.	Have students choose a country and dramatize being a local; then, have the class "travel" around the world talking to the different people. Students analyze propaganda and then plan and act out a part of history where it was used on the populace.

Table 5.1   Teaching Content Through the Arts (Continued)

Discipline	Visual Arts	Dance/Movement	Music	Drama
	values of the United States. Students will compare a painting depicting hatmakers at work to a portrait of a noblewoman of leisure. Next, pupils will write narratives from the perspectives of the women depicted in the paintings and then create a paper hat.			
Language Arts	Have students engage in a guided drawing, followed by writing a description of the drawing. Have students create an adjective tree on a bulletin board and add visual words as leaves throughout the year. Have students display an art piece, provide guiding questions (wonderings/ noticings/ questions/	Parts of a story can be learned with body parts: beginning (head), middle (stomach), and end (toes). In groups, have students select a scene from a piece of literature read in class and create a tableau.	Use songs to teach academic vocabulary. Have students write a story or poem inspired by music. Have students work in groups and use jingles to teach persuasive argument. Have students write an editorial on a song.	Students take on the role of a character and sit in the hot seat, where they answer classmates' questions (e.g., if a student is the wolf, classmates can ask, "Why did you eat the little pigs?"). Create a tableau: Students can develop a still, silent performance

(Continued)

Table 5.1 Teaching Content Through the Arts (Continued)

Discipline	Visual Arts	Dance/ Movement	Music	Drama
	thoughts/ knowledge), then have students use their answers to build a narrative writing piece. Have students choose a literary work and create an abstract painting that depicts the emotional tone of the book.			from a scene in a story or representing an event in text.
Math	Have students explore circumference and diameter by creating an abstract design with a circle. Have students create a colored pencil drawing utilizing lines of symmetry.	Have students explore symmetry through dance.	Have students use videos/ songs to learn to skip count, do number bonds, etc. Music has a natural beat. The visualization of music allows for comprehension of dividing and multiplying fractions. Mathematical formulas for sound waves and vibrations can be learned with tuning forks and understanding that the number of vibrations have varying movement per second.	Students will engage in dramatic play to simulate a cultural marketplace where they will buy and sell goods. Have students compose a math poem and perform a dramatic reading of it. Have students interview a math concept. Have students write simple scenes to illustrate a math concept.

SUPERPOWERED RESOURCES

Additional resources (websites, videos, and books/articles) for boosting long-term memory are provided in this section.

 ## Websites

Free Graphic Organizer Sites

- Learning Disabilities Association of America (LDA)

https://bit.ly/47dObwv

- Canva

https://bit.ly/47hYrE3

- HMH

https://bit.ly/3FZUnMQ

 ## Videos

- **The Powerful Effects of Drawing on Learning**

https://bit.ly/47xoc2R

- **Using Movement to Teach Vocabulary**

https://bit.ly/40DNt9q

 ## Articles/Books

- **Using Music During Instruction to Support Cognition**

https://bit.ly/49CkGpN

- **3 Common Myths About Learning—and What Teachers Can Do Instead**

https://bit.ly/49yRMa5

- Bates, K. E., Gilligan-Lee, K., & Farran, E. K. (2021). Reimagining mathematics: The role of mental imagery in explaining mathematical calculation skills in childhood. *Mind, Brain, and Education*, *15*, 189–198.

- Brown, P. C. (2014). *Make it stick: The science of successful learning.* Belknap Press.

- Sprenger, M. (2018). *How to teach so students remember.* Association for Supervision and Curriculum Development.

REFERENCES

Agarwal, P. K., Nunes, L. D., & Blunt, J. R. (2021). Retrieval practice consistently benefits student learning: A systematic review of applied research in schools and classrooms. *Educational Psychology Review*, *33*, 1409–1453. https://doi.org/10.1007/s10648-021-09595-9

Bengtsson, S. L., Nagy, Z., Skare, S., Forsman, L., Forssberg, H., & Ullén, F. (2005). Extensive piano practicing has regionally specific effects on white matter development. *Nature Neuroscience*, *8*, 1148–1150. https://doi.org/10.1038/nn1516

Craik, F. I. M., & Watkins, M. J. (1973). The role of rehearsal in short-term memory. *Journal of Verbal Learning and Verbal Behavior*, *12*(6), 599–607.

Dunlosky, J., Rawson, K. A., Marsh, E. J., Nathan, M. J., & Willingham, D. T. (2013). Improving students' learning with effective learning techniques: Promising directions from cognitive and educational psychology. *Psychological Science in the Public Interest*, *14*(1), 4–58. https://doi.org/10.1177/1529100612453266

Ebbinghaus, H. (1964). *Memory: A contribution to experimental psychology.* Dover.

Hagan, S. (2012). The mind's eye. *Rochester Review*, *74*(4), 32–37. https://www.rochester.edu/pr/Review/V74N4/0402_brainscience.html

Hasson, U. (2016). What happens in the brain when we hear stories? [Video]. In Ted Conferences. https://www.ted.com/talks/uri_hasson_this_is_your_brain_on_communication

Hattie, J. (2008). *Visible learning*. Routledge.

Heath, C., & Heath, D. (2018, January 10). *The secret to student engagement*. Education Week [Commentary]. https://www.edweek.org/leadership/opinion-the-secret-to-student-engagement/2018/01

Immordino-Yang, M. H., Darling-Hammond, L., & Krone, C. R. (2019). Nurturing nature: How brain development is inherently social and emotional, and what this means for education. *Educational Psychologist*, *54*(3), 185–204. https://doi.org/10.1080/00461520.2019.1633924

Learning Disabilities Association of America. (n.d.). *Graphic organizers*. https://ldaamerica.org/info/graphic-organizers/

Mammarella, N., Fairfield, B., & Di Domenico, A. (2014). Does emotion modulate the efficacy of spaced learning in recognition memory? *Cogent Psychology*, *1*(1). https://doi.org/10.1080/23311908.2014.986922

Marzano, R. J., Pickering, D. J., & Pollock, J. E. (2001). *Classroom instruction that works: Research-based strategies for increasing student achievement*. Association for Supervision and Curriculum Development.

Rinne, L., Gregory, E., Yarmolinskyay, J., & Hardiman, M. (2011). Why arts integration improves long-term retention of content. *Mind, Brain, and Education*, *5*(2), 89–96.

Sprenger, M. (2018). *How to teach so students remember*. Association for Supervision and Curriculum Development.

Sprenger, M. (2019, November 19). *7 brain-based ways to make learning stick*. MiddleWeb. https://www.middleweb.com/37519/7-brain-based-ways-to-make-learning-stick/

Tokuhama-Espinosa, T. N. (2017). *International Delphi panel on mind brain, and education science, 2016 results* [Working paper]. Harvard University Extension School. https://doi.org/10.13140/RG.2.2.14259.22560

Tomlinson, C. A., & Sousa, D. A. (2020). The science of teaching. *Educational Leadership*, *77*, 14–20.

Tullis, J. G. (2023, June 22). *3 common myths about learning—and what teachers can do instead*. Edutopia. https://www.edutopia.org/article/common-myths-learning/

Tyng, C. M., Amin, H. U., Saad, M. N. M., & Malik, A. S. (2017). The influences of emotion on learning and memory. *Frontiers in Psychology*, *8*, 1454. https://doi.org/10.3389/fpsyg.2017.01454

Vlach, H. A., Sandhofer, C. M., & Kornell, N. (2008). The spacing effect in children's memory and category induction. *Cognition*, *109*(1), 163–167. https://doi.org/10.1016/j.cognition.2008.07.013

Whitman, G., & Kelleher, I. (2016). *Neuro-teach: Brain science and the future of education*. Rowman & Littlefield.

ACTIVATING SUPERPOWER

6

TRANSFORMATIVE QUESTIONING

Questions should be an opportunity for dialogue, not monologue.

–Caram and Davis (2005)

A beautiful question is an ambitious yet actionable question that can begin to shift the way we perceive or think about something—and that might serve to bring about a catalyst to bring about change.

–amorebeautifulquestion.com

How many questions do you think a teacher asks on an average school day? The answer may surprise you. It is between 300 and 400 (Levin & Long, 1981). *Questioning* is the second most common routine in which teachers engage. The first, as one could guess, is the lecture. Even though questioning is common-place for teachers, students do not share this nonchalance. For many students, being questioned by the teacher can bring anxiety. This student unease could arise from the very public environment in which questions are usually asked, that is, in front of the whole class with classmates listening to every answer. Using neuroscience as a guide, Chapter 6 will focus on how teachers may transform practices related to traditional classroom questioning into ones for which all students may reap both the learning and the social benefits, making questioning a virtual superpower.

 ## WHAT MAKES QUESTIONING A SUPERPOWER? EXAMINING THE RESEARCH

Most educators are familiar with the pioneering book *Classroom Instruction That Works* (Marzano et al., 2001), which, through a meta-analysis of hundreds of research studies, highlighted nine categories of instructional strategies that effectively improve student achievement across all content areas and grade levels. One of those components is *questioning*. While many teacher questions relate to content and classroom routines, this chapter will focus on those questions aimed at subject matter. Let us examine some of these questioning studies that may superpower your classroom sessions.

NEURO-LINK: Student learning increases when teachers harness the power of questioning. (Marzano et al., 2001; Walsh & Sattes, 2017).

Over the years, countless research studies (Degener & Berne, 2016; Lee & Kinzie, 2012; Morgan & Saxton, 1991; Walsh & Sattes, 2017; Wilen, 1986) have examined the many dimensions of questioning in K–12 classrooms (e.g., higher-order, opportunity to respond [OTR], convergent/divergent). One common trait of all these investigations has been the search for efficacy: How does this questioning routine best promote student learning?

Walsh and Sattes (2017) have identified these kinds of questions as *quality questions*. Quality questions, they claim, have the following four critical traits: they

1. focus students on important content aligned with standards and learning goals,
2. promote one or more carefully defined instructional purposes,
3. facilitate thinking at an appropriate cognitive level, [and]
4. are clearly and concisely worded so that students understand what is being asked. (p. 27)

NEURO-LINK: Questioning sessions that allow students more opportunities to respond (OTR) have been correlated with students' positive academic and behavioral outcomes (Harbour et al., 2015).

Why is this OTR component so essential? From earlier chapters in this text, we learned from neuroscience that when more input channels (visual, auditory, kinesthetic, tactile) are activated, information has a higher chance of moving into long-term memory storage. In most classroom questioning sessions, most students use just a single modality, listening, as they passively perceive the interchange between the teacher and other students. To prove this point, you may recognize the following question prompt that is universal in classrooms today, "Who can tell me…?" or "Who knows…?" Learning increases when teachers modify their routines and move to a questioning dynamic requiring each student to answer all the questions. When the brain responds orally to each question that the teacher asks (as in partner talk) or is required to write answers to each question (e.g., on individual whiteboards), more dendrites are activated, and memory is increased. (See next section in the chapter for classroom ideas of ways to increase opportunities to respond [OTR] for all students.)

NEURO-LINK: Questions that are interesting to students engage them more completely in the learning segment (Caram & Davis, 2005; Cano et al., 2014; Smart & Marshall, 2013).

It seems quite logical that *interesting questions* would be more effective than, let's say, boring ones. Then, what would make a question interesting? Caram and Davis (2005) impart this distinction, "questions that stretch students' minds—the kind that invites students' curiosity, provoke thinking, and instill in students a sense of wonder—keep students engaged" (cited in Able & Fraumeni, p. 23). Smart and Marshall (2013) cited the research support for inquiry-oriented questions as a "potentially integral subcomponent to achieving effective classroom discourse" (p. 250).

Finally, Cano et al. (2014) shared supporting evidence for increased learning when teachers allow students to ask questions. Two elements are in play here. First, when students ask a question, they have a vested interest in the topic. Second, one can only ask a question with some level of comprehension regarding the topic. For example, if you were tasked with devising a question about the propulsion system for the SpaceX rocket, you would need to have background knowledge (comprehension) of rocketry. Similarly, asking students to write questions motivates them to read and assimilate prior information (perhaps from their textbook) that results in deeper comprehension.

In case your interest in SpaceX rockets has been piqued, I am enclosing background information that you might find interesting:

> *Merlin is a family of rocket engines developed by SpaceX for use on its Falcon 1, Falcon 9 and Falcon Heavy launch vehicles. Merlin engines use a rocket grade kerosene (RP-1) and liquid oxygen as rocket propellants in a gas-generator power cycle.*

(SpaceX Merlin, 2023, para. 1)

 NEURO-LINK: Specific types of questions may accelerate neural branching (Caram & Davis, 2005; Cano et al., 2014; Smart & Marshall, 2013).

In a somewhat older study, Cardellichio and Field (1997) found that higher-order questions can increase dendritic branching in the brain. Most teachers are familiar with Bloom's classic and widely utilized taxonomy of educational objectives (1956) and Webb's Depth of Knowledge (1999). However, countless other questioning types can accelerate neural branching. A few of Cardellichio and Field's (1997) examples include the following:

- *Hypothetical thinking* asks students to consider "what if" scenarios, which create opportunities to make new connections in their brain.

- *Analogy* is a powerful way to have students use something they know to help them understand something new. An example would be, *How is the brain like an airport?*

- *Analysis of point-of-view* questions requires students to put themselves in someone else's shoes and consider another viewpoint, thus extending their own brain's frame of reference.

- *Completion* requires students to create a different ending to a story, a moment in history, or an artistic action, which, once again, expands the brain. (para. 7)

USING THIS SUPERPOWER IN YOUR CLASSROOM

Becoming a Master Questioner

Very few teachers have been schooled in the art of questioning. Earlier in the chapter, experts were cited as they weighed in on several dynamics to which master questioners need to attend:

- Giving all students equal opportunities to respond (OTR)
- Ensuring questions are engaging and interesting for students
- Using a variety of question types

Classroom examples for each will be provided in the following section.

Questioning Strategies for Equity: Opportunities to Respond (OTR)

- *Call on students at random*: Write student names on popsicle sticks or ordinary playing cards and draw randomly to call on students, or use a digital random number generator to call on students, allowing more students to respond.

- *Partner talk*: Have students talk with a partner, thereby allowing every student to answer every question. Pre-assign student partners for a set period (weekly/monthly).

- *Turn-and-talk*: Direct students to locate a partner sitting near them (e.g., elbow partners, desk partners).

- *Appointment clocks*: At the beginning of the year, give each student a piece of paper with a clock and times drawn (use hours 1 through 12). Instruct students to roam around the classroom and ask (12) classmates to sign their clock, one for each hour. Note: Once a student signs, let's say, for a 2:00 time slot, on a classmate's "clock," both must put each other's names at the 2:00 time slot. A teacher can say, "Find your 2:00 and share your thoughts."

- *Individual whiteboards* are standard in many U.S. classrooms. These allow all students to "show what they know" simultaneously as they use markers to write their responses to teacher questions.

- *Choral response* has been used in classrooms for over 100 years. This technique allows all students to simultaneously respond as they "call out" an answer. Even if the teacher cannot ascertain individual answers, each child is using another channel in their brain (oral response) to strengthen dendritic branching. A good follow-up would be to prompt students with the "correct" response and have them repeat the choral response several more times. Note: This strategy works best with primary-age students.

- *Individual response cards*
  - » Yes/No or True/False: Simple note cards or sticky notes may be used for Yes/No or True/False questions with one card with YES and another with NO. The teacher asks a question, and students are prompted to hold up either the Yes or NO card (or TRUE/FALSE). After all the students have responded, the teacher may initiate a deeper discussion and ask, "Why is this false?"
  - » Multiple Choice: Again, simple note cards may be used with a letter designating a multiple choice (A, B, or C). The teacher (or a student designee) asks a question with three possible answers, and students hold up either the A, B, or C card.

- *Whole class response:* Students may be given a sticky note to post their response to a teacher's question on the large classroom whiteboard, bulletin board, or chart paper.

- *Digital student response*: Digital apps allow all students to be prompted to choose an answer on their device and respond. Anonymous responses can be visually represented on the screen, or teachers may use them privately for formative assessments. Teachers can then hold a deeper discussion on the topic at hand. Some of these include:

» Digital apps (e.g., Pear Deck, Jamboard, Quizlet) allow students to answer the teacher's questions anonymously via digital apps that display responses on a projection screen for all to see.

» Clickers are digital devices much like a TV remote. Each student clicks to respond to the teacher's questions in a multiple-choice format. Anonymous responses are visually presented on screen.

- *Finger/hand responses* (e.g., Thumbs-up)

- *Four corners*: A teacher designates each of the four corners of the classroom as a possible answer choice to a question. All students are instructed to get up and stand in the corner of the room that corresponds to their chosen answer (e.g., Which character in the story displayed the most courage? Choices: Corner #1, Matt; Corner #2, Attean, Corner #3, Saknis, Corner #4, Matt's Father)

- *Utilizing student questions:* The Right Question Institute developed a unique questioning protocol, the question formulation technique (QFT), to make students comfortable asking questions. To start, a teacher sets a timer for a short time (e.g., 3 minutes) and instructs students to (silently) write as many questions as possible within that time frame. No talking or censuring is allowed. All questions are accepted. Students may write on individual paper or chart paper shared by the group. Once the time is up, different things may happen. The teacher may ask students to work with classmates to nominate three questions for the class to study. Alternatively, the teacher may ask students to classify questions (e.g., convergent/divergent, by levels according to Bloom, etc.)

Questioning to Capture Student Interest

- *Using centers or stations as question motivators:* Centers and stations are used by many teachers. Centers are specialized topics or interest areas where students may choose to work. Stations are similar, except all students rotate to each station either in a class period or during the week. These non-teacher-directed areas allow students to engage in activities that help them to apply new knowledge. Teachers may post key questions at centers and stations for students to answer in groups, in hard copy, or in digital journals. Alternatively, teachers may invite students to develop questions at each center/station for class discussion.

- *Charting:* Having students work on chart paper (or group-sized whiteboards) on desktops increases student engagement in discussing and answering questions. Here are some additional ways this could take place:

» *Vertical charting:* An idea shared in a video (included in the resources section for this chapter) had the teacher assign students to groups, give each group a large piece of chart paper, and ask them to post it on the wall or bulletin board. At the same time, they stood around and discussed various answers to questions posed by the teacher. The authors of this novel approach comment on students feeling more comfortable answering questions and sharing their ideas when freed from their desktops. Also, they recommend (randomized) group roles for each student: (1) the scribe, the only one who may write on the chart; (2) the speaker, who shares the groups' responses during the debrief; (3) the inquirer, who is the only one who may ask the teacher questions; and (4) the manager, who keeps everyone in the group on task.

» *Digital charting:* There are now many digital apps that allow teachers to have students post their responses to questions on digital spaces (e.g., Padlet, Jamboard, Poll Everywhere, Mentimeter)

- *Circle talk:* This is one of my favorite questioning protocols. Circle talk is similar to a class meeting format but is intended for students to answer content-related questions. Students sit in a circle and, in turn, respond to each question posed by the teacher (or even a classmate). There are two rules for circle talk, which add to its effectiveness. One rule is once a question is asked, each student, in turn, gets a chance to answer. This element is essential because students who are more reluctant to answer questions or who need help to think of an answer quickly enough now have a moment that is all theirs, and no interruptions are allowed. The second rule is that students have a right to pass. This rule is potent as when teachers ask a student a question, they either must respond or appear defiant. The "pass" rule allows their emotional safety in choosing not to respond. While some students may initially test their teacher on the pass rule, most start to feel safe in the class to respond when it is their turn on the circle. Once all students have either responded or chosen to pass, the leader may call for *crosstalk,* which invites anyone to comment about another classmate's response or ask a question of them all in front of the entire circle.

Questioning to Open Students' Minds

At the heart of what we do, don't we genuinely aspire to facilitate the opening of students' minds? In the 1990s, Deborah Meier founded 21st Century Schools, a network for public schools serving underprivileged students in New York City and Boston. She is considered one of the most influential educators in the United States. Her central goal for her students was to teach them to think for themselves. While directing Boston's Mission Hills Schools, she developed foundational questions called the "five habits of mind" (Meier, 2009). Teachers were encouraged to integrate these questions into lesson plans. "Having students critically think about what they are learning will provide them with the essential skills to be successful in their future" (2011). I will share them here as they are an exquisite example of the power of questions.

- Evidence (How do I know what is true?)

- Perspective (Who might think differently?)

- Connections (What other areas of knowledge are connected?)

- Supposition (How might it be different if…?)

- Significance (Is this important?)

Questioning Strategies, Especially for Secondary Students

- **Question Stations:** Set up different stations in the classroom, each with a different question or problem. Students rotate through the stations, discussing and solving the questions collaboratively.

- **Case Studies:** Present real-life case studies and ask students to analyze and discuss the situation. They can formulate questions about what they need to know to solve the case.

SUPERPOWERED RESOURCES

 **Websites**

- Wonderopolis

https://wonderopolis.org/wonders

Wonderopolis is an informational site that asks and answers interesting questions about the world. Each day the site poses an intriguing question and then explores it in different ways. The learning that occurs promotes student curiosity, imagination, and creativity. Students also have the chance to submit their own wondering for it to have the chance to be nominated.

- The Right Question Institute

https://rightquestion.org/about/

The Right Question Institute is a nonprofit organization that works to assist all people to ask better questions. They created the question formulation technique (QFT) that is in use in classrooms all over the world. Their site has videos that showcase QFT lessons in elementary, middle, and high school classrooms.

- Classroom Response Systems – The Complete Guide + Top 6 Modern Platforms

https://bit.ly/3MJyHrM

This site is a comprehensive give (with embedded links) to a world of digital apps to use for classroom questioning.

- Project Zero's Core Thinking Routines

https://bit.ly/3SGBExf

A special mention should be made for Project Zero, a 50+ year initiative from the Harvard Graduate School of Education. *The Core Thinking Routines* are one of their most notable accomplishments for their simplicity and because they promote a culture of thinking within classrooms. The site hosts a multitude of question prompts in 10 different categories.

 Videos

- **60-Second Strategy: Class Participation Spinner**

https://bit.ly/47vvQL3

Books/Articles

- **Teaching Through Asking Rather Than Telling**

https://bit.ly/49v3S49

- **Are Questions the Answer?**

https://bit.ly/49MsHJ0

- **3 Strategies to Get All Students Participating**

https://edut.to/3ulEJIO

REFERENCES

Bloom, B. S. (1956). *Taxonomy of educational objectives: The classification of educational goals*. Longmans, Green.

Cano, F., García, Á., Berbén, A. B. G., & Justicia, F. (2014). Science learning: A path analysis of its links with reading comprehension, question-asking in class and science achievement. *International Journal of Science Education*, *36*(10), 1710–1732.

Caram, C. A., & Davis, P. D. (2005). Inviting student engagement with questioning. *Kappa Delta Pi Record*, *42*(1), 19–23. https://www.tandfonline.com/doi/abs/10.1080/00228958.2005.10532080

Cardellichio, T., & Field, W. (1997). Seven strategies that encourage neural branching. *Educational Leadership*, *54*, 33–36.

Degener, S., & Berne, J. (2016). Complex questions promote complex thinking. *The Reading Teacher*, *70*(5), 595–599. International Literacy Association.

Harbour, K. E., Evanovich, L. L., Sweigart, C. A., & Hughes, L. E. (2015). A brief review of effective teaching practices that maximize student engagement. *Preventing School Failure: Alternative Education for Children and Youth*, *59*(1), 5–13. https://www.tandfonline.com/doi/abs/10.1080/1045988X.2014.919136

Lee, Y., & Kinzie, M. B. (2012). Teacher question and student response with regard to cognition and language use. *Instructional Science: An International Journal of the Learning Sciences*, *40*(6), 857–874.

Levin, T., & Long, R. (1981). *Effective instruction*. Association for Supervision and Curriculum Development.

Marzano, R. J., Pickering, D. J., & Pollock, J. E. (2001). *Classroom instruction that works: Research-based strategies for increasing student achievement*. Association for Supervision and Curriculum Development. https://www.marzanoresearch.com/masterful-questioners-harness-the-power-of-questioning

Meier, D. (2009, May). Democracy at risk. *Educational Leadership*, *66*(8), 45–49.

Meier, D. (2011). *5 habits of mind*. https://21centuryschools.wordpress.com/2011/06/28/5-habits-of-mind-debroah-meier/

Morgan, N., & Saxton, J. (1991). *Teaching questioning and learning*. Routledge.

Smart, J. B., & Marshall, J. C. (2013). Interactions between classroom discourse, teacher questioning, and student cognitive engagement in middle school science. *Journal of Science Teacher Education*, *24*(2), 249–267. https://doi.org/10.1007/s10972-012-9297-9

SpaceX Merlin. (2023, December 7). Wikipedia. https://en.wikipedia.org/wiki/SpaceX_Merlin

Walsh, J. A., & Sattes, B. D. (2017). *Quality questioning: Research-based practice to engage every learner* (2nd ed.). Corwin.

Webb, N. (1999). *Webb's depth of knowledge guide*. http://www.aps.edu/rda/documents/resources/Webbs_DOK_Guide.pdf

Wilen, W. W. (1986). *Questioning skills, for teachers*. National Education Association.

NOTES

TRANSFORMING ASSESSMENTS INTO LEARNING OPPORTUNITIES (LOPPS)

*If you really want to see how innovative a school is,
inquire about its thinking and practices regarding assessment.*

–Hardiman and Whitman (2014)

*Research in cognitive science and psychology shows that testing, done right,
can be an exceptionally effective way to learn.*

–Paul (2015)

*I think that's one of the things that the kids don't really like, is doing the reflecting,
but I think it's actually one of the things that helps us a lot.*

–A student (2020)

Assessments are among the most important aspects of teachers' lessons and students' learning. Chapter 7 will explore the changing landscape of assessments, including the potency of renaming summative assessments as *learning opportunities*, the power of formative assessments, and the untapped learning potential of student self-assessment.

WHAT MAKES ASSESSMENT A SUPERPOWER: EXAMINING THE RESEARCH

Assessments play a crucial role in gauging student progress and guiding instructional decisions. They go beyond measuring mere knowledge recall and aim to assess students' understanding, application, and critical thinking skills.

Formative assessments, such as quizzes, class discussions, and observations of student seat-work practice, provide valuable feedback during the learning process that allows educators to adjust instruction accordingly. Summative assessments, such as exams or final projects, measure overall learning outcomes. When assessments are designed to align with learning objectives, provide constructive feedback, and promote reflection, they can be powerful tools for nurturing growth and improving student learning.

 NEURO-LINK: Retrieving information from memory, as compared with simply rereading it, makes the brain work harder and leads to longer lasting memory (Anamalai & Yatim, 2019; Haebig et al., 2021; Paul, 2015).

Through educational neuroscience, a new assessment paradigm is emerging that reveals that the act of testing, itself, can promote learning. The secret to this phenomenon rests in what is called "retrieval practice." In the more popular vernacular, we call this "use it or lose it." How does this phenomenon work? Paul (2015) sheds some light on this by explaining how technology has given us some additional clues about what happens in the brain during the assessment process:

> *Studies employing functional magnetic resonance imaging of the brain are beginning to reveal the neural mechanisms behind the testing effect.… In the handful of studies that have been conducted so far, scientists have found that calling up information from memory, as compared with simply restudying it, produces higher levels of activity in particular areas of the brain. (p. 54)*

We will now examine this testing effect through the lens of both formative assessments (during learning) and summative assessments (at the end of the learning segment).

Summative Assessment

This will be on the test at the end of the week. This oft-used teacher reminder echoes in our collective memories of school. In fact, just hearing the word *TEST* may evoke unpleasant memories for most adults. What if testing was not perceived as the dreaded school practice it currently is? What if testing could be seen as a learning opportunity? One innovative teacher highlighted in Whitman and Kelleher's remarkably informative book *Neuroteach: Brain Science and the Future of Education* (2016) has renamed his summative tests as *learning opportunities* or *LOPPS*. "But this requires educators to think more holistically about assessments to look at ways in which research should inform how students should prepare for a LOPP, take a LOPP, and reflect on their LOPP performance" (pp. 97–98). Although not using the term *learning opportunity*, Dr. Judy Willis speaks to their power as a motivator of student effort. Using the analogy of video games, she observes, "Games insert players at their achievable challenge level and reward player effort and practice with acknowledgment of incremental goal progress, not just final product. The fuel for this process is the pleasure experience related to the release of dopamine" (Willis, 2011, para. 1). Furthermore, she contends that with this dopamine release, students are very willing to try to beat their last score and continue on their quest to master the "game."

Along with the motivation factor, another element is at play in employing the superpower of retrieval practice, what has now been determined to be the most effective method for improving retention. Paul (2015) maintains, "Retrieval practice is especially powerful compared with students' most favored study strategies: highlighting and rereading their notes and textbooks, practices that a recent review found to be among the least effective" (para. 15). Support for this claim is found in a study reported by Karpicke and Roediger (2008). They observed students using two different study techniques for an upcoming vocabulary quiz. One group studied the words by reading and rereading them silently to themselves. The other group studied by self-testing. The group who did the self-quizzing remembered 80% of the words later compared to only 33% remembered by the group who studied by rereading.

Haebig et al. (2021) move this argument forward: "Within the impressive retrieval practice studies that have been documented in the literature, it has become clear that the act of attempting to retrieve information facilitates learning" (p. 3196). Other researchers have theorized that the act of retrieval, itself, may signal the brain to keep the information close at hand, so to speak. "Retrieval practice is an easily implemented learning strategy that is important in supporting and enhancing long-term retention and promoting the transfer of learning" (Anamalai & Yatim, 2019, p. 62).

Formative Assessment

In the past two decades, formative assessments have garnered the attention of countless educational researchers. A classic and groundbreaking meta-analysis by Black and Wiliam (1998) of 250 different research studies uncovered the immense power of formative assessments. They concluded that for teachers who used formative assessments, student gains were "among the largest ever reported for educational interventions" (p. 61). However, it has only been in the last decade that schools have fully embraced these tools. You could even call them *"the new kid on the block"* regarding school district professional development efforts. As we have shared, formative assessments are not new. They are not novel. They are not hard to do. They do not take a great deal of extra time and planning. Why, then, are they just now getting so much attention? Prashanti and Ramnarayan (2019) share one of the reasons for this renewed interest in formative assessments: "Today, the shift in emphasis from summative to formative assessments is the offshoot of the acknowledgment that assessment is as powerful in causing learning as it is in measuring worth" (p. 99). Moreover, esteemed Stanford researcher Linda Darling-Hammond (2015) asserts, "One of the strongest, positive influences on achievement occurs when students get formative feedback that they can immediately apply" (2:37).

Additionally, formative assessments can provide significant rewards for both teachers and students. For teachers, they are an immediate indicator of whether students have learned the content. For students, they are a yardstick of their own learning at a particular point in time, which can motivate them to continue their efforts to reach the finish line.

 NEURO-LINK: Student self-assessment has been proven to be among the most significant influences on student learning and academic success (Bingham et al., 2010; Hudesman et al., 2013).

Self-assessment, in all forms, inspires learners to own their learning. Further-more, self-assessment builds the crucial executive skills of metacognition and self-monitoring (Black & Wiliam, 2009; Clark, 2012). Providing students with the added knowledge that they can change their brains by improving their approach can be a game-changer (Willis, 2009, para. 4).

Reflection and metacognition are powerful tools that promote deep learning and self-awareness. When students reflect, they actively think about their learning processes, evaluate their progress, and identify areas for growth. Metacognition involves being aware of one's own thinking and learning strategies. Through reflection, students develop a deeper understanding of concepts, make connec-tions, and transfer knowledge to real-world situations. Additionally, metacognition enhances problem-solving skills and equips students with strategies to regulate their learning. Stanton et al. (2021) highlight the importance of metacognition, or students' awareness and control of their own thinking, in the learning process and provide recommendations and strategies for educators to consider promoting metacognition in their students. Furthermore, they assert that metacognition is a great predictor of student success. Strong metacognitive skills can help students identify concepts they do not understand, determine appropriate strategies for learning these concepts, implement them, and evaluate their success, adjusting if necessary. By fostering a culture of reflection and metacognition, educators empower students to become self-directed learners who can continually improve their learning outcomes.

In more practical studies, Wilburne and Dause (2017) found that students' levels of perseverance can be improved with instruction in the executive functioning skills of goal-setting and self-monitoring, both components of self-assessment.

 NEURO-LINK: Errors can cause the brain to grow new synapses and, ultimately, assist long-term learning (Boaler, 2013; Hajcak, 2012; Overbye et al., 2020; Pan et al., 2020).

As everyone knows, assessments, especially summative assessments, inevitably come with errors. Neuroscience is shedding light on this seemingly unpleasant phenomenon, which may have a silver lining. "*Errorful learning*—that is, generating errors and subsequently receiving correct answer feedback—can lead to better memory for correct information than errorless learning (Pan et al., 2020, p. 1105). Boaler (2013) adds the neuroscience explanation for this phenomenon: "When students think about why something is wrong, new synaptic connections are sparked that cause the brain to grow.… Students and teachers should value mistakes and move from viewing them as learning failures to viewing them as learning achievements" (p. 149).

This discovery of the brain's ability to grow new synapses after making a mistake is why pretesting is such a powerful learning component. The goal of a pretest is to uncover both what is and what is not known about a topic. When the brain encounters what is unknown, aka a mistake, it tends to work harder to figure out why. This brain activity can create more connections and, thus, opportunities for correct memories to form. Of course, this only happens when the student is invested in the learning in the first place.

An interesting side note emerges regarding how several other nations manage student errors. For instance, Pan et al. (2020) observed the following, "American teachers tend to minimize or deemphasize students' errors, Italian teachers tend to be overtly critical of errors, and Japanese and Chinese teachers often have a positive attitude toward errors and devote substantial amounts of time to discussing them with their students" (p. 1106).

USING THIS SUPERPOWER IN YOUR CLASSROOM

Assessment of student learning is one of the most fundamental responsibilities of a teacher. How we go about this charge is one of our CEO powers. If we choose, we can reframe assessments as *learning opportunities* and, in so doing, allow students more ownership in their own learning. Let's examine three different ways to infuse LOPPS into your classroom routines: (1) formative assessments, (2) alternative summative assessments, (3) student self-assessment, including error-analysis.

Fantastic Formative Assessments

Clearly, formative assessments are regarded as a high-impact practice in schools today. Prashanti and Ramnarayan (2019) give us 10 reasons why this may be so. They also had a bit of fun with alliteration in the process. They are:

1. *Faceless*: The fact that formative assessments are largely anonymous is a big plus for students as they do not feel they will be exposed to their classmates with an incorrect answer.

2. *Facilitates active learning:* Participating in formative assessments is an active process for students. As was stated in earlier chapters, dendrites grow from active experiences as opposed to passive ones.

3. *Feedback:* The feedback component of formative assessments is perhaps THE most critical aspect. Feedback is for the teacher, yes, but also for students to see where they are on the learning continuum.

4. *Feedforward:* And, unlike summative assessments where the feedback is the culmination of learning, feedback in formative assessments fuels additional learning.

5. *Focus on learning:* The focus on learning, as opposed to grading, is one of its most powerful aspects.

6. *Flexibility:* Formative assessments are exceedingly flexible. As will be shared in the resources section, there are literally dozens of ideas for teachers to access for formative assessments from the very simple hand signals to more involved annotated notes on student learning.

7. *Fast:* Easily connected to flexibility is the speed at which a formative assessment can be given: A teacher can request a quick whiteboard response in less than 1 minute.

8. *Frequent:* To be valid, formative assessments need to be given often as learning can change from day to day.

9. *Friendly environment:* Instead of paraphrasing, I will quote the authors directly here as they have articulated this idea in such a reader-friendly manner. "Formative assessments not only instill confidence in the students but also bring about a cultural change in the classroom environment… creating a healthy, safe and supportive environment" (p. 1010).

10. *Fun:* Formative assessments are not your grandmother's tests. They are almost game-like in their enjoyment factor and a welcome break from the more traditional aspects of lesson delivery.

Examples of Formative Assessments: The best thing about formative assessments is that they do not need to be complicated. Even the simplest ones can be very effective. A comprehensive listing of formative assessments is contained in the resources section of this chapter. This listing includes an article by Finley ("Dipsticks: Efficient Ways to Check for Understanding") highlighting 54 ways to formatively assess students and Dye's inclusion of links to over 75 digital tools and apps teachers can use to support formative assessment in the classroom ("75 Digital Tools and Apps Teachers Use to Support Classroom Assessment").

Alternative Summative Assessments

There are two main types of alternative summative assessments: performance and portfolio.

- *Performance assessments* require students to demonstrate their learning by producing an observable product. Examples include the following:
  » Performing a play, debate, or mock trial
  » Exhibits and presentations
  » Projects
  » Concept maps
  » Employing the visual or digital arts, for example, an infographic
  » An engineering design challenge product
  » Flipbook
  » Digital: blogs, comic creator, postcard creator
- *Portfolio assessments* are student work collections highlighting student selection and reflection in entries. Portfolios can be in hard-copy folders or digitally created and content-specific (i.e., math, science, essays) or contain work from various disciplines to showcase what has been learned during a grading period or for parent/caregiver conferences.

Self-Assessments

Neuroscience validates the learning power of self-reflection (which includes metacognition) and self-assessment, where we view our errors as stepping stones to understanding.

- *Journals* are a superb way to engage students in self-reflection as they are cumulative and can document learning growth over time. They also are private as they are shared only with the teacher, allowing students to feel safe in revealing what they've learned.

- *Conferences* allow students one-on-one time with the teacher to self-reflect on their learning progress, discuss challenges, and create new goals.

- *Highlighting errors* instead of correcting them on student homework and assessments allows students, individually and in work groups, to engage in productive self-reflection and learn from mistakes. (See video, Highlighting Mistakes, in resources section).

SUPERPOWERED RESOURCES

 Websites

- Top Tech Tools for Formative Assessment

https://bit.ly/3G18zoS

This site showcases many websites that can be accessed for formative assessments.

 Videos

- **Student Self-Assessment: Reflections From Students and Teachers**

https://bit.ly/47QsAdJ

- **Highlighting Mistakes— A Grading Strategy**

https://bit.ly/3QHclIZ

 Books/Articles

- **Having Students Lead Parent Conferences**

https://bit.ly/3QvVzw0

- **Travel Journals as Student Portfolios**

https://bit.ly/3MIzAkK

- Assessing Students as They Play

https://bit.ly/3R04JCK

- Dipsticks: Efficient Ways to Check Understanding

https://bit.ly/3SFSdJy

- 13 Creative Ways to Do Formative Assessments

https://bit.ly/3SNHGvU

- A Restorative Approach to Grading

https://bit.ly/47dZEfJ

75 Digital Tools and Apps Teachers Use to Support Classroom Assessment. https://www.nwea.org/blog/2021/75-digital-tools-apps-teachers-use-to-support-classroom-formative-assessment/

REFERENCES

Anamalai, T. R., & Yatim, M. H. M. (2019). A comparative study of formative assessment tools. *Journal of Information System and Technology Management*, *4*(14), 61–71. https://doi.org/10.35631/jistm.414006

Bingham, G., Holbrook, T., & Meyers, L. E. (2010). Using self-assessments in elementary classrooms. *Phi Delta Kappa International*, *91*(5), 59–61.

Black, P., & Wiliam, D. (1998). Assessment and classroom learning. *Assessment in Education*, *5*(1), 7–74.

Black, P., & Wiliam, D. (2009). Developing the theory of formative assessment. *Educational Assessment, Evaluation, and Accountability*, *21*(1), 5–31.

Boaler, J. (2013). Ability and mathematics: The mindset revolution that is reshaping Education. *FORUM: For Promoting 3–19 Comprehensive Education*, *55*(1), 143–152.

Clark, I. (2012). Formative assessment: Assessment is for self-regulated learning. *Educational Psychology Review*, *24*, 205–249.

Darling-Hammond, L. (2015, March 25). The five keys to comprehensive assessment [Video]. Edutopia. https://www.edutopia.org/video/five-keys-comprehensive-assessment/

Haebig, E., Leonard, L. B., Deevy, P., Schumaker, J., Karpicke, J. D., & Weber, C. (2021). The neural underpinnings of processing newly taught semantic information: The role of retrieval practice. *Journal of Speech, Language, and Hearing Research*, *64*(8), 3195–3211. https://doi.org/10.1044/2021_JSLHR-20-00485

Hajcak, G. (2012). What we've learned from mistakes: Insights from error-related brain activity. *Current Directions in Psychological Science*, *21*, 101–106. https://doi.org/10.1177/0963721412436809

Hardiman, M., & Whitman, G. (2014, Winter). *Assessment and the learning brain.* National Association of Independent Schools. https://www.nais.org/magazine/independent-school/winter-2014/assessment-and-the-learning-brain/

Hudesman, B. J., Crosby, S., Flugman, B., Issac, S., Everson, H., & Clay, D. B. (2013). Using formative assessment and metacognition to improve student achievement. *Journal of Developmental Education*, *37*(1), 2–13.

Karpicke, J. D., & Roediger, H. L. (2008). The critical importance of retrieval for learning. *Science*, *319*(5865), 966–968.

Overbye, K., Bøen, R., Huster, R., & Tamnes, C. (2020). Learning from mistakes: How does the brain handle errors? *Frontiers for Young Minds*, *8*, Article 80. https//:doi.org/10.3389/frym.2020.00080

Pan, S., Sana, F., Samani, J., Cooke, J., & Kim, J. A. (2020). Learning from errors: Students' and instructors' practices, attitudes, and beliefs. *Memory*, *28*(9), 1105–1122. https://doi.org/10.1080/09658211.2020.1815790

Paul, A. M. (2015). A new vision for testing. *Scientific American*, *313*(2), 54–61. https://doi.org/10.1038/scientificamerican0815-54

Prashanti, E., & Ramnarayan, K. (2019). Ten maxims of formative assessment. *Advances in Physiology Education*, *43*(2), 99–102. https://doi.org/10.1152/advan.00173.2018

Stanton, J. D., Sebesta, A. J., & Dunlosky, J. (2021). Fostering metacognition to support student learning and performance. *CBE Life Sciences Education*, *20*(2). https://doi.org/10.1187/cbe.20-12-0289

Whitman, G., & Kelleher, I. (2016). *Neuroteach: Brain science and the future of education*. Rowman & Littlefield.

Wilburne, J. M., & Dause, E. (2017). Teaching self-regulated learning strategies to low-achieving fourth-grade students to enhance their perseverance in mathematical problem-solving. *Investigations in Mathematics Learning*, *9*(1), 38–52.

Willis, J. (2009, December). *How to teach students about the brain*. Educational Leadership. http://www.radteach.com/page1/page8/page44/page44.html

Willis, J. (2011, April). A neurologist makes the case for the video game model as a learning tool. Edutopia. https://www.edutopia.org/blog/neurologist-makes-case-video-game-model-learning-tool

SPARKING THE BRAIN'S CREATIVE FORCES

What makes someone successful in the 21st century is definitely not your ability to memorize facts. What will make someone successful is your relentless capacity to innovate, to create.

–Zhao (2012)

While watching students define creativity, I was struck by how much in agreement

I was with them at its basic definition—creativity is imagination or ideas.

–A teacher (2019)

By now, almost all U.S. educators have heard of the 4 C's of the 21st-century skills, that is, communication, collaboration, critical thinking, and creativity. This last area, creativity, may be the least addressed in classrooms today. One reason may be the association of creativity exclusively with the arts. Yes, it does reside there. However, it also exists in countless examples of everyday thinking and problem-solving. Educational neuroscience informs us that learning something through creative means or divergent thinking is more likely to stick. That is precisely how teaching for creativity can become a superpower. Chapter 8 will invite teachers to consider a broader view of creativity beyond the arts, including decision-making, problem-solving, and design-thinking.

DEFINING CREATIVITY

Before we examine how the brain fosters our creative abilities, it would be useful to first define creativity. Though experts do not agree on one definition, in its simplest terms, most subscribe to the idea that creativity is related to having novel thoughts or ideas. The noted psychologist J. P. Guilford is thought to be the grandfather of creativity. Guilford is credited with adding the concept of divergent thinking to creativity. According to Guilford (1967), divergent thinking involves "the ability to generate multiple solutions to a situation or problem" (cited in "Divergent and Convergent Thinking," n.d.).

Sir Ken Robinson is an internationally known creativity expert and is passionate about the need for creativity to be prioritized in classrooms today. Robinson defines creativity as "having original ideas that have value." Incidentally, his presentation, listed in the resources at the end of this chapter, holds first place as the most-watched Ted Talk video of all time with almost 75 million views. That fact validates how much people value creativity.

Abraham Maslow adds an essential element to this discussion: creativity within all of us. "Creativity is a fundamental characteristic, inherent in human nature, a potentiality given to all or most human beings at birth, which is often lost or buried or inhibited as the person gets enculturated" (Maslow, 1968, as cited in Starko, 2018, p. 57). Considering all these definitions, if creativity is the experience we have when we experience novel thoughts or ideas, then everyone has creative capacity. Using that logic, what might creativity look like in school? Starko (2018) offers this interpretation: "If students successfully communicate an idea or endeavor to solve a problem, their efforts can be considered appropriate. If they do so in a way that is original, at least to them, we can consider the efforts creative" (p. 14).

Beaty et al. (2019) argue that creativity is more than just relegated to the arts. It is a part of all life.

> *Creative thinking is central to the arts, sciences, and everyday life. How does the brain produce creative thought? A series of recently published papers have begun to provide insight into this question, reporting a strikingly similar pattern of brain activity and connectivity across a range of creative tasks and domains, from divergent thinking to poetry composition to musical improvisation.*
>
> **(Beaty et al., 2019, p. 87)**

Have you ever had an idea for a new…

- route when you are stopped in traffic?
- ingredient in a recipe?
- way to solve a work-related problem?
- way to put clothes together for an "outfit"?
- _____ (fill in the blank)?

Yes, everyone has had untold numbers of these large and small occurrences. While the modern world is increasingly unpredictable and our challenges are unprecedented, teachers must understand creativity and how it can be nurtured in the classroom to prepare the next generation with the skills they will need to succeed. Furthermore, in the face of recent events in our nation and worldwide, it is even more self-evident that our classrooms need to be a place where creative and compassionate thought is nurtured as an indispensable component in developing an enlightened, tolerant, and engaged society.

CREATIVE TEACHING VERSUS TEACHING FOR CREATIVITY

I would like to make a claim that ALL teachers are creative! I am not only referring to the engaging lessons we design but also to the hundreds of ways we creatively and flexibly adapt to the unplanned occurrences in our classrooms every single day. And, while it is always desirable for teachers to use our creative abilities, your superpower resides more in how you may *facilitate the natural inborn creativity of your learners.* To underscore this last point, Starko (2018) asserts, "The difference between teaching for creativity versus creative teaching concerns the "opportunities for originality among the students" (p. 20).

WHAT MAKES CREATIVITY A SUPERPOWER? EXAMINING THE RESEARCH

As educators prepare students to work and live in the 21st century's globally focused society, we must be aware of the skills that students will be required to possess to be truly successful within such a society. In an oft-cited study conducted by IBM, CEOs from numerous nations and industries were surveyed on what they view as the most essential leadership qualities for employees today. Though there was a disparity in many categories between the views of North American CEOs and those of other global regions, about 60% of all of the CEOs polled cited creativity as the most critical leadership quality (Carr, 2010). Perhaps, this is one reason why starting in 2022, in addition to the basics of reading, mathematics, and science, creativity is now being measured by the Program for International Student Assessment (PISA), an international assessment for 15-year-olds every 3 years. On the creativity assessment, PISA "will examine students' capacities to generate diverse and original ideas and to evaluate and improve ideas, across a range of contexts or 'domains'" (OECD, n.d., para. 2).

 NEURO-LINK: Certain specific neurotransmitters have been identified with creativity (Zhang et al., 2021).

The brain's chemical transmitters affect creative thinking in large and small ways. Three neurotransmitters within the brain influence creative thinking: serotonin, dopamine, and the neuropeptide oxytocin. This information, pinpointing the chemical signature of creative thinking, is an astounding advance in neurology. Furthermore, most importantly, these neurotransmitters exist in every human brain.

 NEURO-LINK: Creative thought is a synthesis of several distinct areas of the brain (Beaty et al., 2015; Koontz, 2019).

The interplay of different brain networks involved in creative thinking has led researchers to create these three labels: the imagination network, where daydreaming and brainstorming happen; the central executive network which allows us to pay attention to a complex task; and the salience network, which involves speech and language (Beaty et al., 2015; Koontz, 2019).

Dr. John Kounios has studied what happens in the brain before one has a creative insight or "aha" moment. He says insight is not instantaneous but begins with an idea in the unconscious mind. An exciting action occurs just before the moment of insight. The back of the brain blinks. Alpha waves shut down the visual cortex for a millisecond to limit distractions and allow the brain to find and retrieve subconscious ideas. This "blinking" allows ideas to surface to the conscious level in a flash of insight (Kounios & Beeman, 2009).

Now let us focus on the front part of the brain, the prefrontal cortex. The frontal lobes are the "gatekeepers" of creativity. The frontal lobes control executive functioning. When we are undergoing creative exercises, it is more likely that the frontal lobes are in a dreamlike state, allowing us to be less inhibited and take risks, diverging from the known to new unexplored areas and having a more creatively receptive mind.

 NEURO-LINK: Creative thought originates in both right and left hemispheres of the brain (Beaty et al., 2019; Whitman & Kelleher, 2016).

In the 1980s, the construct of the right/left brain came into vogue in popular culture. The left hemisphere was (supposedly) our logical-thinking side and the right hemisphere was (again, supposedly) where creativity was situated. Neuroscientists have thoroughly debunked this theory and moved this unsubstantiated "right/left brain" theory into popular brain mythology. Now, it has been well established that human creativity exists in both hemispheres and is an intricate interchange using the entire brain (Beaty et al., 2019). This advance in understanding has been made possible by brain imaging techniques. While it is true that the right hemisphere of the brain is associated with creative thought, it is essential to realize creativity is a function that happens between both hemispheres.

 NEURO-LINK: To maximize students' creative thinking, the size of group work matters (Amichai-Hamburger et al., 2016; Kim, 2019; Luo et al., 2023; Qiu & McDougall, 2015; Shaw, 2013; Yang et al., 2022).

There are advantages and disadvantages to various group sizes. Large groups (10+) and medium groups (5+) may generate more creative ideas; however, there is a greater chance of student nonparticipation and staying on the sidelines (Amichai-Hamburger et al., 2016; Qiu & McDougall, 2015). Small groups (pairs, triads, and quads) provide more safety to individuals, but personal relationships may influence group dynamics (Kim, 2019; Yang et al., 2022). Researchers have concluded that the evidence supports small groups over medium or large ones in supporting students' experiences, including creative thinking (Luo et al., 2023; Shaw, 2013).

USING THIS SUPERPOWER IN YOUR CLASSROOM

When teachers arrange the teaching day so that students have abundant opportunities to flex their creative thinking, their creativity self-efficacy can more easily emerge. Creativity self-efficacy is the belief in one's ability to produce creative ideas, solutions, or performance (Yeh et al., 2023).

Class Discussions

First, student participation is an absolute necessity if the goal is to teach for creativity. This participation may take many forms—oral, written, or using visuals such as drawing or graphic organizers. Let us start with one of the daily occurrences in classroom discussions. In elementary classrooms, many students vie for the opportunity to share their thoughts. In middle and high schools, not so much. As participation is necessary for students to practice and develop their creative abilities, how might this student engagement be accomplished?

I want to share a metaphor that has stayed with me for several decades. Years ago, I attended an educational presentation at a conference on classroom discussions. The speaker spoke of a phenomenon researchers observed in classrooms during most discussions. The data revealed that, on average, only about seven students regularly answered questions that teachers posed. (Now, if you are a secondary teacher, you might be thrilled to find even seven students who willingly share their thoughts in class.)

The speaker labeled this trend "The Magnificent 7," after the well-known movie in 1960. Furthermore, he stated that, if pressed, teachers and students could easily identify those seven, with students, more than likely, believing that these classmates were the smart/creative ones in class. I have confirmed this claim informally in my teacher education courses. Each semester, when I approach the topic of equity during class discussion, I ask my preservice teachers, who all participate in required fieldwork in schools, if they see a regular group of students called upon much more frequently than their peers. Just about everyone raises their hands in affirmation that they have seen this phenomenon in their practicums. (Note: I did commence a digital search to see if I could find this individual's remarks, only to discover that many writers have now co-opted the term *Magnificent 7* to describe all manner of good teaching practices.)

Let us examine ways to counter the "Mag 7" in the classroom. First, look back to classroom tips on engaging students (Chapter 2) and powerful questioning (Chapter 7). Next, let's examine how creativity may be enhanced in ordinary daily activities of class discussions.

Whole Class Discussions

Whole class discussions have many advantages, including an inclusive environment for everyone in the class, community sharing of ideas, and bringing full-class attention to the topic at hand. When using whole class discussions to engage students' creative thinking, consider these ideas:

- Before starting the discussion, introduce the topic and invite all students to add some ideas on sticky notes to affix to chart paper or the class whiteboard.

- Use a digital app (Poll Everywhere or Jamboard) and invite students to add their ideas anonymously. Use student ideas and have students expand them.

- Have each student take one idea that a classmate provided and change it in some way (e.g., add to it, agree or disagree with it, and provide reasons).

- Teacher picks several responses randomly, reads them to the class, and asks, "What would happen if this were to be fact?"

Small Groups and Pairs

It may seem obvious, but for most children and adults, speaking in smaller groups is less intimidating than speaking in larger ones. "Research indicates that pairs contribute equally to the process of collaboration, have more opportunities to participate, and can concentrate on ideas without being influenced by other members" (Dugosh et al., 2000). Building collaborative group work into lessons will encourage lesson participation and bring out less confident pupils' creative ideas and contributions.

Divergent Thinking

Once students feel safe participating in classroom discussions, then, specific creative thinking structures may be added to the mix. Divergent thinking is one of them. There are four main ways to facilitate divergent thinking: flexibility (variety of ideas), elaboration (development of an idea, fluency (number of ideas), and novelty (unique ideas) (Starko, 2018).

1. Flexibility: Have students generate different hypotheses for (a) an action of a character in a story, (b) a solution to a math problem, and (c) an action in a science lab. Post all the hypotheses (on chart paper, on whiteboard, or digitally). Students will be more likely to engage to see which hypothesis is the correct one.

2. Elaboration: In groups, have students work to discover how something works, for example, (a) government, (b) an oil rig, (c) a computer, (d) a skateboard. Have a student from each group report to the whole group.

3. Fluency: Brainstorming is the process of generating many ideas in a short amount of time. Most adults have had many opportunities for this creative endeavor. However, brainstorming is rarely done in school as part of content lessons with students. The reason may be that, as teachers, we first think of the content knowledge in a lesson. A slight variation would be to ask, "Is there a place in this lesson where it would be helpful for students to produce many ideas"? If the answer is "yes," then a group setting may be preferable as it is generally experienced by students as playful and not as threatening due to the brainstorming dictum "there are no bad ideas." Just that one rule allows talkers and non-talkers alike to take a chance and offer ideas. Figure 8.1 highlights the many benefits of having students participate in brainstorming sessions in the classroom.

Figure 8.1 Brainstorming Benefits for Students

1. *Encourages student engagement:* The playful feeling of brainstorming, where there are *no bad ideas,* immediately gets students involved.
2. *Provides teachers with a sense of students' prior knowledge:* Brains love to make associations, a key cognitive action. Brainstorming gives teachers a sense of the prior knowledge that their students bring to the lesson.

3. *Enhances students' collaborative skills:* Though brainstorming can certainly be done in isolation, a synergy is experienced when collaborating with others and building on each other's thinking.
4. *Highlights misunderstandings:* Even as the brainstorming rule indicates that all ideas are accepted, a teacher can use this time to uncover any misconceptions students may bring to the experience and correct those during subsequent lessons.
5. *Increases students' willingness to speak up:* An added energy can often be experienced during a brainstorming session. Students feel that as well, and many are swept up in the activity and forget their former reluctance to share their ideas in front of their classmates.

Following are some examples of brainstorming that can be used with each content discipline.

Mathematics: Can we think of all the ways that rectangles and squares are alike?

Science: Name all the ways patterns can be observed in nature or energy in nature. Note: The Crosscutting Concepts from the Next Generation Science Standards (NGSS) provide an excellent backdrop for countless brainstorming opportunities. The seven Crosscutting Concepts are:

1. *Patterns*
2. *Cause and effect*
3. *Scale, proportion, and quantity*
4. *Systems and system models*
5. *Energy and matter*
6. *Structure and function*
7. *Stability and change*

(National Research Council, 2012, pp. 84–85)

Language Arts: Brainstorming analogies can be done by kindergartners and 12th graders alike. The teacher merely writes the prompt, "How is ____like ____?" For younger students, this might take the form of "How is a book like an adventure?" or "A friend is like….." Older students can be given only the first part of an analogy to complete with the second part. After they do, then, instruct them to come up with three similarities. For example, offer the prompt, "The brain is like" and have the students finish the sentence with what they think the brain is like (e.g., roots on a tree, an orchestra, a spider web, a forest, air traffic control, a computer).

Social Studies: The acronym GPS is a useful tool for brainstorming ideas for history/social studies. G stands for geographical, P for political, and S for social/cultural. Almost any person or historical event may be viewed through these three lenses. Let's use George Washington. Have students brainstorm facts that they know about America's first president. Once a list is generated, have groups categorize the facts and place them under each heading (i.e., geographical, political, or social/cultural.) Another example could be the event of the California Gold Rush. Again, have students brainstorm ideas for the California Gold Rush with GPS (geographical, political, and social/cultural).

Design-Thinking

Design-thinking is not just for engineering; it is a creative way for humans to solve problems. There are many design-thinking models, but all are quite similar. In "NASA for Kids: Intro to Engineering" (https://www.youtube.com/watch?v=wE-z_TJyzil&t=1s), this sequence includes the following:

- ASK: Identify the problem, requirements that must be met, and constraints that must be considered.
- IMAGINE: Brainstorm solutions and research ideas, including what others have done.
- PLAN: Make a plan by consulting several of the most useful ideas gleaned from brainstorming and choosing a design.
- CREATE: Build a working model.
- TEST: Evaluate the solution through testing; collect and analyze data; summarize strengths and weaknesses of the design that were revealed during testing.
- IMPROVE: Based on the results of tests, make improvements.

You will note that each one of the steps requires creative thought. Also, these steps could be used in a wide variety of situations (making a paper airplane that would stay in the air for a long time, creating a pet play area, planning a trip, collecting rainwater, designing a game, creating something to carry a large package, etc.).

Augmenting Student Creativity Through the Visual and Performing Arts: Visual, Musical, Dance, and Drama

At the beginning of this chapter, it was clear that creativity is not solely consigned to the arts. However, adding the arts as an ingredient to enrich content instruction may be another pathway to teach creativity and, thus, enhance

Figure 8.2   Design-Thinking Steps

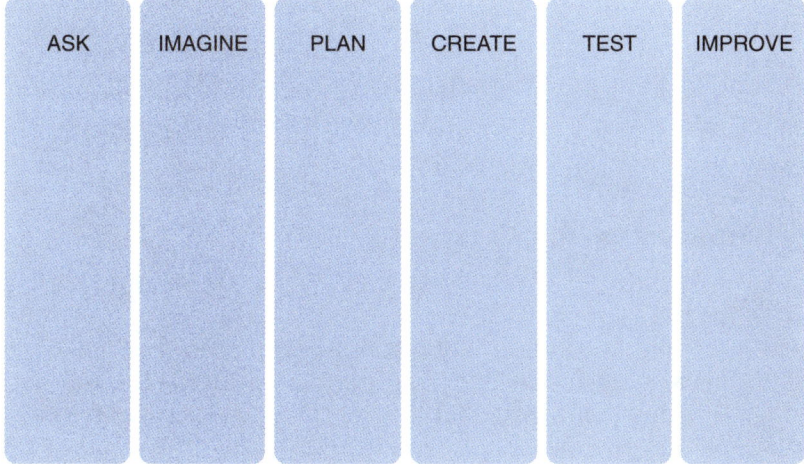

ASK	IMAGINE	PLAN	CREATE	TEST	IMPROVE

Source: Adapted from NASA, https://www.youtube.com/watch?v=wE-z_TJyzil&t=1s

students' creative self-efficacy. See Chapter 5 for teaching ideas that integrate the visual arts, dance/movement, music, and drama into each major content discipline.

SUPERPOWERED RESOURCES

🖥 Websites

• The University of Pittsburgh Center for Creativity

https://www.creative.pitt.edu/

This robust university-sponsored website holds many resources for teachers at all levels.

• Drexel University: Creativity in the Classroom

https://bit.ly/47r0A04

Drexel University showcases the many benefits to students for adding creativity-inspired elements to daily lessons.

Videos

- Changing Education Paradigms

https://bit.ly/40DHMsa

- Creativity 21st Century Skill

https://bit.ly/47g2l03

This classic video by Sir Ken Robinson, a world-renowned education and creativity expert, questions our standard educational approach and emphasizes that divergent thinking comes naturally, whereas our current paradigm stifles it.

 Books/Articles

- Using Visual Facilitation Strategies in Small Group Discussions

https://edut.to/3R3Hg3C

- Science Takes Flight With Paper Airplanes

https://edut.to/40MhGDq

- Tips for Guiding Students to Think Creatively

https://bit.ly/3sGKQab

- 4 Myths About Creativity

https://bit.ly/3SEOagD

- 5 Techniques to Promote Divergent Thinking

https://bit.ly/47eLSJw

- Cultivating Creativity in Standards-Based Classrooms

https://bit.ly/3MMc2v0

- **Why Integrating Art Into the Classroom May Improve Content Retention**

https://bit.ly/3sC3MqK

This article provides a solid research base for adding the arts into classroom instruction.

REFERENCES

Amichai-Hamburger, Y., Gazit, T., Bar-Ilan, J., Perez, O., Aharony, N., Bronstein, J., & Dyne, T. S. (2016). Psychological factors behind the lack of participation in online discussions. *Computers in Human Behavior*, *55*, 268–277. https://doi.org/10.1016/j.chb.2015.09.009

Beaty, R. E., Benedek, M., Kaufman, S. B., & Silvia, P. J. (2015). Default and executive network coupling supports creative idea production. *Scientific Reports*, *5*, 10964.

Beaty, R. E., Seli, P., & Schacter, D. L. (2019). Network neuroscience of creative cognition: Mapping cognitive mechanisms and individual differences in the creative brain. *Current Opinion in Behavioral Sciences*, *27*, 22–30.

Carr, A. (2010, May 18). The most important leadership quality for CEOs? Creativity. *Fast Company*. http://www.fastcompany.com/1648943/creativity-the-most-important-leadership-quality-for-ceos-study

Divergent and convergent thinking. (n.d.). Design4Services. https://design4services.com/concepts/divergent-and-convergent-thinking/

Dugosh, K. L., Paulus, P. B., Roland, E. J., & Yang H.-C. (2000). Cognitive stimulation in brainstorming. *Journal of Personality and Social Psychology*, *79*, 722–735. https://doi.org/10.1037/0022-3514.79.5.722

Kim, K. H. (2019). Demystifying creativity: What creativity isn't and is? *Roeper Review*, *41*(2), 119–128. https://doi.org/10.1080/02783193.2019.1585397

Koontz, A. (2019, March). The circuitry of creativity: How our brains innovate thinking. *Cal Tech Letters*.

Kounios, J., & Beeman, M. (2009). The aha! moment: The cognitive neuroscience of insight. *Current Directions in Psychological Science*, *18*(4), 210–216.

Luo, H., Chen, Y., Chen, T., Koszalka, T. A., & Feng, Q. (2023). Impact of role assignment and group size on asynchronous online discussion: An experimental study. *Computers and Education, 192*, 104658. https://doi.org/10.1016/j.compedu.2022.104658

National Research Council. (2012). *A framework for K-12 science education: Practices, crosscutting concepts, and core ideas*. National Academies Press. https://doi.org/10.17226/13165

Organisation for Economic and Co-operative Development (OECD). (n.d.). *PISA 2022 creative thinking*. https://www.oecd.org/pisa/innovation/creative-thinking/

Qiu, M., & McDougall, D. (2015). Influence of group configuration on online discourse reading. *Computing Education, 87*, 151–165. https://doi.org/10.1016/j.compedu.2015.04.006

Shaw, R.-S. (2013). The relationships among group size, participation, and performance of programming language learning supported with online forums. *Computers and Education, 62*, 196–207. https://doi.org/10.1016/j.compedu.2012.11.001

Starko, A. J. (2018). *Creativity in the classroom: Schools of curious delight* (6th ed.). Routledge.

Yang, T., Luo, H., & Sun, D. (2022). Investigating the combined effects of group size and group composition in online discussion. *Active Learning in Higher Education*, *23*, 115–128. https://doi.org/10.1177/1469787420938524

Yeh, Y., Ting, Y.-S., & Chiang, J.-L. (2023). Influences of growth mindset, fixed mindset, grit, and self-determination on self-efficacy in game-based creativity learning. *Educational Technology & Society*, *26*(1), 62–78.

Whitman, G., & Kelleher, I. (2016). *NeuroTeach: Brain science and the future of education*. Rowman & Littlefield.

Zhang, Q., Yun, K., Wang, H., Yoon, S., & Lu, F. (2021). Automatic cell counting from stimulated Raman imaging using deep learning. *PLoS One*, *16*(7), e0254586.

Zhao, Y. (2012). *World class learners: Educating creative and entrepreneurial students*. Corwin Press.

NOTES

PROMOTING CULTURALLY RESPONSIVE AND RELEVANT TEACHING

Do the best you can until you know better. Then when you know better, do better.

–Maya Angelou

Culturally responsive teaching is grounded in social and cognitive neuroscience.

–Zaretta Hammond (2015)

When classroom data show that there are patterns to which students we are not reaching, patterns predictable by race, class, gender, or home language,

it can set off the amygdala upstairs.

–Jill Harrison Berg (2020)

We all have a cultural background. It matters to us. Now, we are learning how aspects of culture have been encoded into our brains. Culturally responsive/ culturally relevant pedagogies add an extra layer of support to how we learn. If our dendrites are formed from our experiences, our cultural background looms large in forming our brain's entire structure. This fact is true for all students, not just students of color, and it affects student achievement, self-efficacy, and graduation rates. This chapter will address the brain principles underlying why culturally responsive/culturally sustaining teaching is effective and its critical importance in meeting the needs of our growing culturally, racially, ethnically, and linguistically diverse student body.

WHAT MAKES CULTURALLY RESPONSIVE AND RELEVANT TEACHING A SUPERPOWER? EXAMINING THE RESEARCH

An emerging field of study, cultural neuroscience, involves studying the inter-action between culture and the brain. This interdisciplinary field aims to investigate how culture might affect the underlying brain pathways of each member of the culture (Kitayama & Park, 2010). From these and other researchers, we learn that teachers' intentional decisions to teach in culturally appropriate ways can access and support powerful brain–culture linkages, which, in turn, may supercharge their instruction.

Enter *culturally responsive teaching*, a term first used in the 1990s by Gloria Ladson-Billings (1992), a professor at the University of Wisconsin. Since then, other academics have proposed corresponding terminology to this domain to widen the scope. These more recent terms are *culturally relevant teaching* and *culturally sustaining teaching*. Dr. Matthew Lynch (2012) defined *culturally responsive teaching* as "a student-centered approach to teaching in which the students' unique cultural strengths are identified and nurtured to promote student achievement and a sense of well-being about the student's cultural place in the world" (para. 2). Lynch identifies three separate dimensions. The first dimension, the institutional dimension, recognizes "the need for reforming the cultural factors affecting the organization of schools, school policies and procedures (including the allocation of funds and resources), and community involvement" (para. 3). The second dimension, the personal dimension, refers to "how teachers learn to become culturally responsive" (para. 3). And the third dimension, the instructional dimension, refers to "practices and challenges associated with implementing cultural responsiveness in the classroom" (para. 3). We will now examine the third dimension—instructional—through the lens of neuroscience.

 NEURO-LINK: Cultural experience is encoded in our brain (Earley & Ang, 2003; Freeman et al., 2009; Han & Northoff, 2009; Hedden et al., 2008; Kitayama & Park, 2010; Zhou & Fischer, 2013).

Zhou and Fischer's (2013) research in neuroscience led to an astounding fact: "Cultural experience and learning sculpts the anatomy and function of the human brain and shapes human behavior" (p. 227). As a result of this research, a new interdisciplinary field, cultural neuroscience, was born to study the interconnec-tions among culture, mind, and the brain. "This emerging field of research aspires to understand how culture as an amalgam of values, meanings, conventions, and artifacts that constitute daily social realities might interact with the mind and its underlying brain pathways of each member of the culture" (Kitayama & Park, 2010, p. 111). This connection of culture and the brain is primarily due to the plasticity of the human brain and the brain's dendritic branching, which differs in humans as a result of our cultural upbringing. In this paper, the researchers point out how cultural experience is encoded into the brain and the way in which it processes information. For example, bicultural students can respond in two ways: having blended and alternating bicultural identities. These differing identities can be seen affecting how their brains process information. Thus, it is essential that teachers teach in culturally appropriate ways to reach their students. From their deep analyses of the literature, Zhou and Fischer (2013) conclude, "Successful educational reform and pedagogy require that teachers become culturally and neuroscientifically literate" (p. 229).

 NEURO-LINK: Culturally responsive/sustaining pedagogies assist students in building intellective capacity and intellective competence (Hammond, 2015).

Hammond (2015) asserts that culturally responsive/sustaining practices are not a "bag of tricks" for teachers to use mainly to motivate learners. Instead, when used correctly, these practices have the power to change the brain through intellective capacity, or "the increased power the brain creates to process complex information more effectively" (p. 16). The brains of learners grow more competent through these practices. This input from neuroscience is quite astounding and provides further motivation for educators to create opportunities to integrate culturally responsive and relevant practices into their classroom routines.

 NEURO-LINK: Cultural relevance is deeply connected to cognitive processing (Hammond, 2015).

Hammond advanced the connections between culture and neuroscience with her influential book, *Culturally Responsive Teaching and the Brain* (2015). Earlier, we examined how strong emotional events imprint on our brains and stay with us long after the event. Hammond builds on this phenomenon and further asserts that the brain depends on culturally shaped perceptions to determine whether emotionally charged interactions—essential to powerful learning—are perceived as threats or opportunities (Berg, 2020). Maintained by the body of research connecting culture to the brain, Hammond (2015) proposed six brain rules for teachers.

1. The brain seeks to minimize social threats and maximize opportunities to connect with others in the community.

2. Positive relationships keep our safety-threat detection system in check.

3. Culture guides how we process information.

4. Attention drives learning.

5. All new information must be coupled with existing funds of knowledge to be learned.

6. The brain physically grows through challenge and stretch, expanding its ability to do more complex thinking and learning (pp. 47–49).

For this chapter, I would like to focus on her third rule: "Culture guides how we process information." She states, "Cultures with a strong oral tradition rely heavily on the brain's social engagement systems to process information. … These elements help build neural pathways and activate myelination" (Hammond, 2015, p. 48). Because her book is so germane to the topic, I have included it in the resources section of this chapter.

 NEURO-LINK: When students feel that classroom work is something that they can comfortably handle (i.e., is within their zone of proximal development), they do not feel as anxious and, thus, are more motivated to tackle it (Baars & Wijnia, 2018; Hammond, 2015; Vygotsky, 1934/1986).

When students perceive that they are supported when tasks appear to be harder, they are more likely to try the task and to identify the experience as pleasurable (Baars & Wijnia, 2018). This statement indeed could be said for all students. However, educational researchers have uncovered a persistent achievement gap for students of color, as this headline indicates from *The 74*, a nonprofit news organization covering America's education system: "America's Achievement Gap—Made, Not Born? A study of 30,000 Students Reveals Lowered Expectations and Poorer-Quality Instruction for Kids of Color." Cantor (2018), the article's author, asserts, "Students of color consistently receive less challenging instruction and schoolwork than do their white and more affluent classmates, a new study has found, often leaving them unprepared for college even if they have received top grades" (para. 1).

To counteract this unrelenting statistic, teachers might reexamine Vygotsky's grounding theory, which stresses that an individual's brain needs new challenges to continue learning. For the best results, these challenges should be marginally ahead of the learner's current ability level. In Chapter 1, you were introduced to the power of teachers' expectations and how students pick up on the spoken and more subtle ways that teachers communicate beliefs in their ability to learn. However, when they understand why we are giving them a challenge, we communicate that we know they can handle it. Moreover, with appropriate scaffolds, often, they rise to the occasion. Hammond (2015) provides some ways teachers may apply Vygotsky's celebrated zone of proximal development to students in today's culturally diverse classrooms.

- Culturally responsive teaching (CRT) builds students' brain power by improving information processing skills using cultural learning tools. Many often relate culturally responsive teaching to affective measures alone. However, with new technology that can uncover the brain's inner workings, neuroscientists can better understand how CRT can provide a cognitive framework to strengthen students' neural pathways.

- Don't equate readiness with ability. Often teachers assume that students in culturally diverse classrooms do not have the ability to learn something when it is simply a factor of their language comprehension.

- Create learning routines that have some flexibility to allow students to work independently with the teacher and with a small group of classmates. This intentional employment of the zone of proximal development provides students with the best of both worlds, targeting instructional time with the teacher and time with other students to learn from and with them.

 ## USING THIS SUPERPOWER IN YOUR CLASSROOM

Creating a Culturally Safe Classroom Environment

In Chapter 2, we discussed the neuroscience behind the necessity of creating an emotionally safe classroom environment for students. Viana (2020) contends this directive is an even greater imperative in a culturally diverse classroom. He suggests the following six classroom practices to support students and, to use a bit of brain speak, keep their amygdala happy.

1. *Tap into culture.* Ask students about their lives and families. Allow students to talk about their cultures and their families' cultures. Include activities in the classroom that celebrate their cultures.

2. *Design visual diversity.* Ensure that students are represented in the materials that are used in the school, including all facets of classroom design. Teachers should ensure that students can see themselves in the presented books, that diversity is represented around the visual

classroom, and that students and families are celebrated in their goals for their students' lives.

3. *Make the classroom student-centered.* A genuinely multicultural classroom requires students to discuss their experiences, traumas, hopes, and dreams.

4. *Pronounce names correctly.* Learn students' names and pronounce them correctly, which makes a considerable difference in validating students' identities.

5. *Set high expectations.* Given the research on the power of teacher expectations, we know that students perform to our expectations of them.

6. *Come from an asset-based mindset.* It is common for teachers to use a deficit-based mindset to evaluate students who lack skills in certain areas.

(Adapted from Viana, 2020, para. 7)

Using Cultural Knowledge as a Scaffold

Connecting new knowledge to what we already know sits at the very core of the principles of how the brain works. From general psychology, these are called schema, "a cognitive framework or concept that helps organize and interpret information" (Cherry, 2023, para. 1). When teachers can access students' cultural reference points, it allows students to comprehend and store new learnings more readily.

At the beginning of the year, have students create a How I Know board with three sections: (1) I know…, (2) I care about…, and (3) I wish people understood that… (Figure 9.1).

Figure 9.1 *How I Know* **Board**

How I Know		
I know…	I care about…	I wish people understood that…

This exercise can be repeated throughout the semester/year as a personal and class reference point.

Variation: The *How I Know* board can easily be used to connect to any content topic that the class is studying.

Enhancing Student Voice Through Projects

In Chapter 4, we discussed the many benefits of project-based learning (PBL). Projects allow students to express their thoughts and have their voices heard. For example, a culture-enhancing driving question, *How can we bring stories to life in our communities?* can open doors to cross-cultural understanding among students and teachers, students and their peers, and schools and their communities. It can also engage students' creativity with a final product promoting their cultural stories. The collaborative discussions challenge students not only to share their ideas but also to question and defend them. Finally, projects involve all four 21st-century skills: critical thinking, creativity, communication, and collaboration.

Other PBL ideas with a cultural variation include

- How may oral histories of unsung heroes in our community bring us a more complete picture of our cultural understanding?

- How can museums (both real and virtual) support our understanding of our cultural heritage?

- How may photographs of our community help us appreciate and recognize different cultural contributions?

SUPERPOWERED RESOURCES

 **Websites**

- Culturally Responsive Hispanic Resources

https://bit.ly/47xlNFA

This site showcases videos, articles, and lesson plans.

- Southern Poverty Law Center: Learning for Justice

https://bit.ly/47cfDux

This renowned organization provides social justice tools for classroom teachers.

- Mathematica: Resources for Culturally Responsive Teaching

https://bit.ly/47vRyyH

This platform is devoted to culturally responsive teaching with a focus on mathematics.

- National Museum of African American History and Culture

https://bit.ly/3MLS0kx

This newest of the Smithsonian Museums provides a comprehensive historical examination of the history of African Americans in the United States.

- Teaching for Change

https://www.teachingforchange.org/

A special focus of this site is a wide-ranging collection of social justice books for elementary and secondary students.

 Videos

- **Teaching for Black Lives**

https://bit.ly/3QZcrNb

- **Learning About Difference and Belonging Through Books**

https://bit.ly/47ebYfX

- **Zaretta Hammond: Culturally Responsive Teaching and the Brain Webinar**

https://bit.ly/49wOVP3

Hear from one of the nation's foremost voices on culturally responsive teaching.

Books/Articles

- Zaretta Hammond: 3 Tips to Make Any Lesson Culturally Responsive

https://bit.ly/3GkPY7r

This article showcases three simple techniques for teachers to include culturally responsive teaching elements in most lessons.

- Teaching for Black Lives by Dyan Watson, Jesse Hagopian, and Wayne Au

https://rethinkingschools.org/ books/teaching-for-black-lives/

- America's Achievement Gap— Made, Not Born? What a Study of 30,000 Students Reveals About Lowered Expectations and Poorer-Quality Instruction for Kids of Color

https://bit.ly/47vRLBZ

- 4 Ways to Build Relationships With Students Whose Backgrounds Differ From Yours

https://bit.ly/3SCSRYt

- Preparing for Cultural Diversity: Resources for Teachers

https://qrs.ly/eafck0p

REFERENCES

Baars, M., & Wijnia, L. (2018). The relation between task-specific motivational profiles and training of self-regulated learning skills. *Learning and Individual Differences*, *64*, 125–137.

Berg, J. H. (2020, May). Learning and the brain. *Educational Leadership*, *77*(8), 86–87.

Cantor, D. (2018, September). *America's achievement gap—Made, not born? What a study of 30,000 students reveals about lowered expectations and poorer-quality instruction for kids of color*. The74. https://www.the74million.org/article/study-achievement-gap-not-inevitable-it-reflects-lower-expectations-poorer-quality-instruction-for-students-of-color/

Cherry, K. (2023, March). *What is a schema in psychology?* Verywellmind. https://www.verywellmind.com/what-is-a-schema-2795873

Earley, P. C., & Ang, S. (2003). *Cultural intelligence: An analysis of individual interactions across cultures*. Stanford University Press.

Freeman, J. B., Rule, N. O., Adams, R. B. J., & Ambady, N. (2009). Culture shapes a mesolimbic response to signals of dominance and subordination that associates with behavior. *NeuroImage*, *47*, 353–359.

Hammond, Z. (2015). *Culturally responsive teaching and the brain*. Corwin.

Han, S., & Northoff, G. (2009). Understanding the self: A cultural neuroscience approach. *Progress in Brain Research*, *178*, 203–212.

Hedden, T., Ketay, S., Aron, A., Markus, H. R., & Gabrieli, J. D. (2008). Cultural influences on neural substrates of attentional control. *Psychological Science*, *19*, 12–17.

Kitayama, S., & Park, J. (2010). Cultural neuroscience of the self: Understanding the social grounding of the brain. *Social Cognitive and Affective Neuroscience*, *5*(2–3), 111–129.

Ladson-Billings, G. (1992). Culturally relevant teaching: The key to making multicultural education work. In C. A. Grant (Ed.), *Research and multicultural education: From margins to the mainstream* (pp. 107–121). Falmer Press.

Lynch, M. (2012, February 13). *What is culturally responsive pedagogy? Huffington Post*. https://www.huffpost.com/entry/culturally-responsive-pedagogy_b_1147364

Viana, J. (2020). 6 Ways to create a culturally responsive classroom. *eSchool News*. https://www.eschoolnews.com/district-management/2020/11/30/6-ways-to-create-a-culturally-responsive-classroom/

Vygotsky, L. (1986). *Thought and language* (A. Kozulin, Ed. & Trans.). MIT Press. (Original work published 1934)

Zhou, J., & Fischer, K. W. (2013). Culturally appropriate education: Insights from educational neuroscience. *Mind, Brain, and Education*, *7*(4), 225–231. https://doi.org/10.1111/mbe.12030

CHAMPIONING NEURODIVERSITY:
VALUING THE SMART IN EVERY STUDENT

If we want to use the most effective approaches with kids—and draw on new research about the brain— special education needs to change its approach.
–Thomas Armstrong (2017)

Neuroscientists have confirmed that each of us has a brain that is unique and has an unfathomable capacity to learn. In this final chapter, I will explain how teachers may embrace neurodiversity and even convert it into a superpower by diversifying ways for learners to receive information, process it, and demonstrate their understanding.

WHAT MAKES NEURODIVERSITY A SUPERPOWER? EXAMINING THE RESEARCH

Neurodiversity. This term may be a harbinger of a profound paradigm shift in special education. Armstrong (2017) gave this insight into the origin of the word: "Coined in the early 1990s by journalist Harvey Blume and Australian autism activist Judy Singer, the term *neurodiversity* can be defined as an understanding that neurological differences are to be honored and respected just like any other human variation, including diversity in race, ethnicity, gender identity, religion, sexual orientation, and so on" (p. 11).

 NEURO-LINK: Each brain is unique (Crossland, 2010; Posey, 2020; Sousa & Tomlinson, 2018).

A fascinating fact about the brain, and the one that is by far the most challenging for teachers, is that every brain is entirely unique. Posey (2020) adds, "Even identical twins have differently active brain patterns and neural networks" (para. 12).

This certainty is acknowledged because the neurons in each of our brains "can be activated or deactivated based on the interactions an individual has with their environment" (para. 12).

 NEURO-LINK: Universal design for learning (UDL) is supported by neuroscience (Posey, 2020).

One of the most exciting new practices in our classrooms is Universal Design for Learning (UDL). The Center for Applied Special Technology (CAST, n.d.) defines UDL as "a framework that guides the design of instructional goals, assessments, methods, and materials that can be customized and adjusted to meet individual needs" (para. 1). UDL's instruction relies on teachers utilizing three guidelines for instruction: (1) multiple means of ways to *engage* learners, (2) multiple means of ways for teachers to *represent* the content, and (3) multiple means of *action and expression* for students to demonstrate their mastery. However, it may not be widely known that UDL practices are directly aligned with neuroscience's understanding of three learning networks in the brain: (1) the recognition networks, (2) strategic networks, and (3) affective networks. Rose and Strangman (2007) define these networks thusly, "Broadly speaking, one component recognizes patterns, a second one plans and generates patterns, and the third one determines which patterns are important. Each of these components is involved, not only in the general act of cognition, but also in specific functions, including memory, language, problem-solving, and thinking" (p. 383).

They assert a parallel between the brain's use of all three networks and UDL's three alternative ways of presenting information to students. With this knowledge, teachers are invited to shift their mindsets and design lessons so that all students' experiences and variabilities are embraced. Posey (2020) observes, "When we provide a 'buffet' so students can select their own pathway to achieve the goals of a lesson, we're aligning instruction more to what we know about the variability of the learning brain" (para. 17). However, Stolz (2023) cautions that UDL is not the whole answer, "Access, though, is more than UDL and more than placement within special or general education settings. It entails giving attention to how students feel and whether they can safely bring their whole selves to the classroom" (p. 73).

 NEURO-LINK: A strengths-based approach is supported by neuroscience (Armstrong, 2017; Diehl et al., 2014; Mottron, 2011).

As educators, we want to support all of our learners. However, in the current IEP-centered special education environment, students diagnosed with learning needs must be classified as disabled to receive specialized services. A newer, neurodiversity-based special education approach sees learner differences as part of the normal human variation, like hair color and handedness. The emerging literature centers on assessing special education populations' strengths, talents, and abilities (Armstrong, 2017). For example, Samson et al. (2012) inform us that the visual processing parts of the brain are more active than speech processing centers in the brains of people with autisms. They conclude by making the thought-provoking assertion that this reallocation of brain activity can still be construed as superior performance.

At this point, I would like to share a comment from a teacher I had in class this last spring. She shared a common occurrence that she observed in IEP meetings that were mostly focused on student deficits. She observed how downtrodden some students feel because they believe they have a "broken" brain. I would like to end this section on a hopeful note. For the past 100 years, we have been teaching *the whole class*. Perhaps in the next 100 years, we will be teaching the *whole student*.

 NEURO-LINK: Technology can be our co-teacher and students' second brain (Naaz et al., 2014; Whitman & Kelleher, 2016).

The widespread availability of electronic devices helps teachers differentiate instruction and allows students to create, interact, and cooperate by using shared documents, word processors, communicative devices, and online discussions. Whitman and Kelleher (2016) offer the following superpowered ways digital technologies can support teaching and learning:

- Technology provides novelty. Mind, brain, and education (MBE) research says that novelty can boost deep, reflective cognitive engagement; it also implies that arts integration can help with motivation and memory preservation, and many of these communication technologies include an artistic component.

- As a research tool, technology can assist in providing students with a strong knowledge base.

- Technology allows for choice and self-agency that provides students the sense that they are in charge of their own learning, which MBE research says might help them stay motivated.

- The diversity of media via which students can communicate ties together with MBE research on the value of teaching and assessing in different modalities that supports differentiation. We are more likely to engage more students and have them use content in ways that will help it "stick" for them if we use a variety of modalities.

- Technology assists students to access, manipulate, and communicate ideas.

USING THIS SUPERPOWER IN YOUR CLASSROOM

The construct of neurodiversity certainly resonates with educators. What an awesome way to describe, well, all of us! Yet, most teachers would agree that a major challenge exists regarding ways to differentiate classroom instruction, considering enormous time limitations, so that each student's and all students' learning needs are met. I do not have an answer to this challenge, but I would like to share a catchphrase that I heard at a conference and now have adapted to fit many different situations in my own life. It is meant to be said (silently) to oneself. It goes like this: "Anything, that I due to _____ (e.g., differentiate instruction for my learners) is better than nothing at all." As I said, I use this for all behaviors that I wish to improve in my professional and/or personal life (healthy eating, exercise, etc.). It allows me to start somewhere and take those first few steps. I offer the following ideas as a place to start actualizing the power of neurodiversity in your classroom.

Empowering Students Through Choice

If teachers can create even a modicum of choice for students, then all students, including those with special needs, would have a say in how they practice and demonstrate their learning that is more compatible with their needs.

Menus

Many teachers use *menu* formats to allow for student choice. These may be posted on the board, and selections may be changed daily on charts in the classroom to denote more general categories for choices (e.g., compose a letter to a Martian giving them a description of what you learned about _____, invent a game that you can practice _____with friends, draw a picture of what you learned about_____. Being more general, these choice boards don't need to change often. You can even use a restaurant-style menu format where each student chooses an *appetizer, main course, and dessert* activity. This last one is especially useful in longer units of study that may last several weeks.

Tic-Tac-Toe

A particularly engaging option for student choice is a 3 × 3 tic-tac-toe, grid-style student worksheet (see Figure 10.1). Students may be instructed to choose one of the nine choice options or even given a full week to require that students practice the skills with several choices during the week.

Figure 10.1   Tic-Tac-Toe Worksheet

Read book	Write a poem	Play a game
Practice with a friend	Draw a picture	Watch a video
Write in journal	Use manipulatives	Write on big chart

Centers

Long employed to incorporate student choice, centers are a staple in many classrooms. Here are three ways to differentiate centers for student needs:

- Create an open-ended activity that students can engage with at different ability levels. For example, you could display several pictures of your teaching topic and have students supply a written description or a comparison between two pictures. Another idea is to have students find one or more similarities or differences between two historical periods, elements on the periodic table, characters in a literature book, math equations, etc.

- Tiered activity games are a way to encourage engagement and allow for different levels of difficulty. For example, the game of Memory involves students finding matches with vocabulary cards as they turn over pairs of cards. The cards can be color-coded into easy, medium, and challenging sets for students to choose.

- Digital activity can use personal devices to access game choices to play with a partner to practice particular skill sets.

Seek Student Input

I recently viewed a video of a teacher who employed a simple coding method at the bottom of every assignment, "This was TOO EASY, JUST RIGHT, A CHALLENGE for me right now." Students circled the response that best fits that assignment. I am aware that complete trust in one's teacher and a classroom environment that includes a "growth mindset" philosophy would need to be in place for something like this to work. However, it seemed like this teacher intended to start "somewhere" in her quest to meet the needs of her students.

Teach Like a Talent Scout: Discover Each Student's Talent

If you have not yet been introduced to Temple Grandin, let me do this now. Dr. Grandin is renowned in two fields: animal husbandry and autism. Identifying as a person with autism, Dr. Grandin presents to international audiences the asset model rather than the deficit model of special education, providing a rationale for contemplating talents that all students come with. A metaphor of *teacher-as-talent-scout* fits nicely here. Employing group work or project-based learning is an ideal way for the teacher (and classmates) to become aware of an individual student's talents and skill sets.

 ## General K–12 Strategies Tailored to Accommodate Neurodiversity

1. **Visual Schedules**

   • Use visual schedules to outline the day's activities. Visual cues help students anticipate transitions and reduce anxiety.

2. **Flexible Grouping**

   • Rotate students through different groupings to cater to various learning preferences.

3. **Sensory-Friendly Environment**

   • Create a calming classroom with soft lighting, fidget tools, and sensory corners where students can retreat if they feel overwhelmed.

4. **Structured Routines**

   • Establish clear and consistent routines. Neurodiverse students often thrive in predictable environments.

5. **Visual Aids and Graphic Organizers**

   • Use visual aids and graphic organizers to break down complex information. Mind maps and diagrams can enhance understanding.

6. **Multisensory Learning**

   • Incorporate hands-on activities and interactive lessons that engage different senses, making learning more accessible.

7. **Social Skills Activities**

   • Organize activities that focus on social skills development, like role-playing, collaborative projects, and peer mentoring.

8. **Storytelling and Creativity**

   • Encourage storytelling and creative expression. These activities allow students to communicate ideas in diverse ways.

9. **Emotional Regulation Techniques**
   - Teach emotional regulation techniques such as deep breathing, mindfulness, and self-reflection. These skills are valuable for all students.

10. **Technology Integration**
   - Use educational apps and software that cater to various learning styles. Some apps are specifically designed for neurodiverse learners.

11. **Peer Support Systems**
   - Implement buddy systems where neurotypical students support neurodiverse peers, fostering understanding and friendship.

12. **Choice Boards**
   - Provide choice boards for assignments and activities. Allowing students to select tasks based on their interests promotes engagement.

13. **Positive Reinforcement**
   - Use positive reinforcement techniques to motivate students. Celebrate achievements and progress, no matter how small.

14. **Collaborative Projects**
   - Plan collaborative projects where students can work together, leveraging each other's strengths and talents.

15. **Regular Check-Ins**
   - Conduct regular check-ins with students to understand their concerns and provide additional support if needed.

16. **Culturally Responsive Teaching**
   - Be aware of cultural differences and incorporate diverse perspectives into the curriculum to create an inclusive learning environment.

17. **Parent and Caregiver Involvement**
   - Involve parents and caregivers in the educational process. Collaborate on strategies that work both at home and in the classroom.

18. **Celebrating Differences**
   - Foster a classroom culture that celebrates neurodiversity. Teach students about different neurological conditions to reduce stigma and promote empathy.

SUPERPOWERED RESOURCES

 Websites

• Buck Institute for Education: PBL Works

https://www.pblworks.org

The Buck Institute is the preeminent PBL site for TK–12 teachers, offering both theory and examples of projects for teachers.

Videos

• An Inspiring Story of a 9-Year-Old and His Belief That His Dyslexia Is His Superpower

https://qrs.ly/pbfck53

• Temple Grandin: The World Needs All Kinds of Minds

https://qrs.ly/hsfck5a

• Teaching Methods for Inspiring the Students of the Future

https://qrs.ly/1efck5e

• Respecting the Differences Between People

https://qrs.ly/vefck5g

• We Are All Different, and That's Awesome!

https://qrs.ly/rlfck5j

 **Books/Articles**

- Creating an Inclusive Classroom for Neurodivergent Learners

  https://qrs.ly/s4fck5q

- Neurodiversity in Maker Space or Classroom

  https://qrs.ly/wpfck5v

REFERENCES

Armstrong, T. (2017, April 1). Neurodiversity: The future of special education? *Educational Leadership*, *74*(7).

CAST. (n.d.). *About universal design for learning*. https://www.cast.org/impact/universal-design-for-learning-udl

Crossland, J. (2010). Brain biology and learning. *School Science Review*, *91*(337), 99–107. https://www.researchgate.net/profile/John-Crossland/publication/234738117_Brain_Biology_and_Learning/links/54e4a53b0cf22703d5befb09/Brain-Biology-and-Learning.pdf

Diehl, J. J., Frost, S. J., Sherman, G., Mencl, W. E., Kurian, A., Molfese, P., Landi, N., Preston, J., Soldan, A., Fulbright, R. K., Rueckl, J. G., Seidenberg, M. S., Hoeft, F., & Pugh, K. R. (2014). Neural correlates of language and non-language visuospatial processing in adolescents with reading disability. *NeuroImage*, *101*, 653–666. https://doi.org/10.1016/j.neuroimage.2014.07.029

Mottron, L. (2011, November 3). Changing perceptions: The power of autism. *Nature*, *479*, 33–35.

Naaz, F., Chariker, J. H., & Pani, J. R. (2014). Computer-based learning: Graphical integration of whole and sectional neuroanatomy improves long-term retention. *Cognition and Instruction*, *32*(1), 44–62. https://www-jstor-org.sandiego.idm.oclc.org/stable/43941135?seq=2

Posey, A. (2020). Leveraging neuroscience in lesson design. *Educational Leadership*, *77*(8). http://www.ascd.org/publications/educational-leadership/may20/vol77/num08/Leveraging-Neuroscience-in-Lesson-Design.aspx

Rose, D. H., & Strangman, N. (2007). Universal design for learning: Meeting the challenge of individual learning differences through a neurocognitive perspective. *Universal Access in the Information Society*, *5*(4), 381–391.

Samson, F., Mottron, L., Soulières, I., & Zeffiro, T. (2012). Enhanced visual functioning in autism: An ALE meta-analysis. *Human Brain Mapping*, *33*, 1553–1581.

Sousa, D. A., & Tomlinson, C. A., (2018). *Differentiation and the brain: How neuroscience supports the learner-friendly classroom* (2nd ed.). ASCD & Solution Tree.

Stolz, S. (2023, May). Building an anti-ableist pedagogy. *Educational Leadership*, *80*(8).

Whitman, G., & Kelleher, I. (2016). *Neuroteach: Brain science and the future of education*. Rowman & Littlefield.

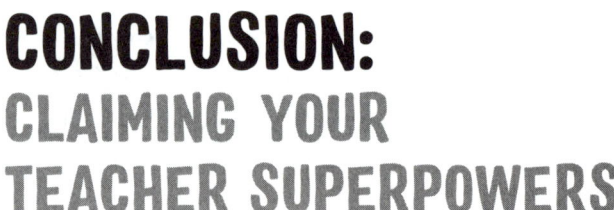

CONCLUSION:
CLAIMING YOUR
TEACHER SUPERPOWERS

In reality, teachers have the most important job in the world.
–"Why Teachers Are Important—Why Teachers Matter," (2023)

The 10 chapters in this book have taken you on a neuro-journey to activate what I have termed your *teacher superpowers*. I labeled them as such because of recent scientific advances from the educational neurosciences regarding the enhanced instructional power of these high-impact practices. Examined through multiple lenses, these superpowers include:

- teaching students about the power of their own brain,

- capturing students' attention and engaging them in the learning segment,

- creating socially and emotionally safe classroom environments,

- supporting students' long-term memory formation in lesson delivery,

- tapping the power of student-to-student collaboration,

- rethinking question-and-answer classroom routines,

- constructing assessments as learning opportunities (LOPPS),

- uncapping the creative spark in all students,

- appreciating how culture shapes learning, and

- showcasing the *smart* in all students.

Perhaps Tokuhama-Espinosa (2010) said it best, "Neuroscientists, psychologists, and educators have studied learning for centuries. It is apparent, however, that while the science of learning is well established, the science of teaching is not as advanced" (p. 11). How, then, can we advance our own instructional growth?

 ## CLAIMING YOUR SUPERPOWERS

I teach education professionals across all levels. One of my favorite courses to teach is what I have termed *the brain course.* As teachers dive into these neuroscience-inspired journeys, I am often asked, "Why didn't my preparation program give me any of this information about the brain?" To respond, let me relay a story of my own growth as an educator. Over the years, as I have learned more effective teaching methods, I often harbored the thought, "Someone surely should have told me about this sooner." Now, after decades of teaching, I have come to treasure what I don't know, as this motivates me to dive in, learn something new, and, thus, reinvigorate my everyday practices and even my life energy.

THE POWER OF LIFELONG LEARNING

Today, as I see myself as a communicator between neuroscience and education, I offer you the same opportunity to reframe these *brain-centered* explorations as opportunities to reimagine aspects of your own instructional routines in some small but powerful ways. There are three reasons this reframing could be helpful:

1. *It keeps you young.* Burnout is an adverse state of being everyone hopes to avoid. Instead of looking forward to going to work each day, you may wake up with feelings of apathy or even dread. Any worker may be susceptible to burnout after years in their field. However, teacher burnout is well-documented in the literature (Bottiani et al., 2019; Herman et al., 2018; Kim & Burić, 2020). As Hurley (2021) asserts, "Teacher burnout has become one of the biggest problems plaguing the education system today" (p. 22).

2. *Learning is natural.* The brain is hardwired to learn. Kwik (2022) communicates this truth thusly, "The fact is, our brain is on a mission from the moment we're born to learn. It's actually programmed to actively seek out new information" (para. 2). We seem to understand, intuitively, that our students have a natural learning instinct. However, we may not often consider that we are imbued with this same drive to learn.

3. *Learning is fun.* Finally, even as adults, we experience learning something new as enjoyable. Could this be because we are no longer in school, and no one is grading us on how much or how fast we learn? I often pause and take in the fact that my hand-held smartphone can transport me anywhere and help me learn anything I choose. In my youth, my family bought the full set of *Encyclopedia Britannica* so that my sister and I could do what my phone now offers me in the blink of an eye. We can now delight in the *joy of learning* as the universe of knowledge is at our fingertips.

Kids and teens spend large portions of time in a school environment where comparisons and judgment are inevitable. Personally, I believe that teaching them about the control they have to change their brain is an empowering motivational skill. And what a wonderful gift to bestow on them that, if they take it in, will keep giving throughout their lifetime.

I would like to end this book, as I did in Chapter 1, with a quote from a teacher.

There is great power when our students know, understand, and value

all the magic within their brains. Let's show them how!

–**A teacher**

REFERENCES

Bottiani, J. H., Duran, C. A. K., Pas, E. T., & Bradshaw, C. P. (2019). Teacher stress and burnout in urban middle schools: Associations with job demands, resources, and effective classroom practices. *Journal of School Psychology*, *77*, 36–51.

Herman, K. C., Hickmon-Rosa, J., & Reinke, W. M. (2018). Empirically derived profiles of teacher stress, burnout, self-efficacy, and coping and associated student outcomes. *Journal of Positive Behavior Interventions*, *20*(2), 90–100. https://doi.org/10.1177/1098300717732066

Hurley, D. (2021). Extinguishing teacher burnout. *Brandon University Journal of Graduate Studies in Education*, *13*(2), 22–27. https://files.eric.ed.gov/fulltext/EJ1173521.pdf

Kim, L. E., & Burić, I. (2020). Teacher self-efficacy and burnout: Determining the directions of prediction through an autoregressive cross-lagged panel model. *Journal of Educational Psychology*, *111*(8), 1–17. https://doi.org/10.1037/edu0000424

Kwik, J. (2022). *The brain loves learning*. Medium. https://kwikbrain.medium.com/3-reasons-the-brain-loves-learning-3b4e6ec66d36#:~:text=The%20fact%20is%2C%20our%20brain,-our%20brain%20happy%20and%20healthy

Tokuhama-Espinosa, T. (2010). *The new science of teaching and learning: Using the best of mind, brain, and education science in the classroom*. Teachers College Press.

Why teachers are important—Why teachers matter. (2023). University of the People. https://www.uopeople.edu/blog/the-importance-of-teachers/#:~:text=Teachers%20have%20the%20ability%20to,important%20job%20in%20the%20world

INDEX

A Sage Company

Helping educators make the greatest impact

CORWIN HAS ONE MISSION: to enhance education through intentional professional learning.

We build long-term relationships with our authors, educators, clients, and associations who partner with us to develop and continuously improve the best evidence-based practices that establish and support lifelong learning.

Solutions YOU WANT | Experts YOU TRUST | Results YOU NEED

INSTITUTES

Corwin Institutes provide regional and virtual events where educators collaborate with peers and learn from industry experts. Prepare to be recharged and motivated!

corwin.com/institutes

ON-SITE PROFESSIONAL LEARNING

Corwin on-site PD is delivered through high-energy keynotes, practical workshops, and custom coaching services designed to support knowledge development and implementation.

www.corwin.com/pd

VIRTUAL PROFESSIONAL LEARNING

Our virtual PD combines live expert facilitation with the flexibility of anytime, anywhere professional learning. See the power of intentionally designed virtual PD.

www.corwin.com/virtualworkshops

CORWIN ONLINE

Online learning designed to engage, inform, challenge, and inspire. Our courses offer practical, classroom-focused instruction that will meet your continuing education needs and enhance your practice.

www.corwinonline.com

Visit **www.corwin.com**

PLSN209A8